HOW TO: GIVE A GREAT PRESENTATION

Neil Chalmers graduated from the University of Manchester with a degree in Politics and American Literature, and went on to spend twenty years in advertising. He worked in the UK and North America as an account handler and board director of the major agencies J. Walter Thompson, Young & Rubicam, KMP and Leo Burnett and, for a period, as a Group Account Director on the board at Saatchi & Saatchi London, where he was responsible for the Conservative Party, Gillette, Courvoisier and Department of Energy accounts.

After leaving Saatchi, Chalmers set up his own communications consultancy with a focus on presentations, speeches and business pitches. He has worked with such clients as Eurotunnel, J. P. Morgan, Bartle Bogle Hegarty, Lowe Howard-Spink, US Surgical, Kleinwort Benson, James Capel, the London Docklands Development Corporation, XL Insurance and The Bank of Bermuda.

how to: ACADEMY launched in September 2013. Since then it has organized over 400 talks and seminars on Business, Lifestyle, and Science & Technology, which have been attended by 40,000 people. The aim of the series is to anticipate the needs of the reader by providing clarity, precision and know-how in an increasingly complex world.

NEIL CHALMERS

HOW TO: GIVE A GREAT PRESENTATION

bluebird
books for life

First published 2016 by Bluebird
an imprint of Pan Macmillan
20 New Wharf Road, London N1 9RR
Associated companies throughout the world
www.panmacmillan.com

ISBN 978-1-5098-1447-3

9 8 7 6 5 4 3 2 1

A CIP catalogue record for this book is available from the British Library.

Illustrations by Dan Colman

Printed and bound by CPI Group (UK) Ltd, Croydon, CR0 4YY

Visit **www.panmacmillan.com** to read more about all our books
and to buy them. You will also find features, author interviews and
news of any author events, and you can sign up for e-newsletters
so that you're always first to hear about our new releases.

Contents

Introduction 1

1: Some Key Principles 9

2: How to Achieve Consistency 23

3: How to Construct Your Presentation 37

4: How to Deliver Your Presentation 58

5: How to Ensure that You Say What You
Want to Say in the Way You Want to Say it 67

6: How to Handle Question-and-Answer Sessions 79

7: How to Make Visual Aids Work for You 91

8: How to Make the Killer Point in Presentations
and Avoid Snatching Defeat from the Jaws
of Victory 101

9: Media Training and Crisis Management 115

Conclusion 129

Useful Organizations 131

Index 133

INTRODUCTION

*'Everything becomes a little different
as soon as it is spoken out loud.'*
Hermann Hesse

Let's begin with a story.

A graduate – we'll call him Tom – goes for an interview with an advertising agency.

Ushered into a meeting room where the walls are covered in cork tiles and the chairs are the most uncomfortable he's ever sat on, he waits for the arrival of his interviewer. As the clock ticks, he rehearses in his head his interview technique and recalls the considerable research he's done into the agency's client list. At last the door bursts open and a human dynamo strides in, with shirtsleeves rolled up, tie loosened, and a steely stare. The dynamo introduces himself as one of the three partners, the first letters of whose names make up the agency's title. Suddenly all Tom's youthful confidence, in place till a moment ago, evaporates.

The interview starts with some quick-fire questions. Why did Tom take his particular degree and what did he find most interesting about it? He's halfway through a lengthy explanation about the difference between two of the writers he studied, when he realizes that the dynamo is staring out of the window, clearly not listening to what he is saying.

Tom now learns something that will stay with him for years to come: that it is essential to make sure his audience is engaged, *all the time*, with what he's saying. Luckily, his interviewer notices Tom's confused silence and asks him to run through once more what he'd just been saying. The result of this unexpected request is that Tom ends up unwittingly digging himself deeper into a hole by speeding up the stumbling account of what he learned on his university course. Taking pity on him, the interviewer suggests that they start again, right from the beginning.

While Tom might have had little idea of what to expect from the interview, his interviewer knew exactly what his own objectives were. It was obvious that Tom had prepared himself, and once he'd calmed down, he was able to answer the questions with considerable insight and enthusiasm. It was easy to see he'd respond well to direction, was willing to learn, and was capable of standing his ground. Tom was offered the job.

But that wasn't the end of his particular learning process. Tom now had to gain and keep the attention of both his colleagues and clients by making sharp and effective presentations. These, he realized, were a vital part of selling the agency's ideas.

A couple of months into his time with the agency, a meeting was called to discuss progress on the design of a number of new products. In his junior capacity, Tom prepared the agenda, booked the meeting room and briefed his boss, who then, to his horror, announced that Tom would be presenting one design because, although he'd only spent a relatively short time at the agency, he'd been the one working closely with the team.

Tom froze. He'd had no time to prepare, he hadn't developed a plan for the presentation and he'd no objectives to work towards: nothing. There was however an actual three-dimensional pack design and, clearly flustered, he started to talk about what the design had tried to do. After thirty seconds or so his speech began to speed up, his mouth took over from his brain and he found himself talking utter rubbish. He realized all too quickly that in the short time he'd been at the agency he hadn't taken on board the skills to do what was now required of him. Sweat began to trickle down his back.

Fast-forward six months. Tom is now making regular presentations and building his confidence. Another review meeting on the projects for which he was responsible is called, attended by the same cast as before, but this time his boss isn't there. The location is the client's offices and so Tom is careful to finish all his planning and preparation for the meeting, including the visuals, the day before. On this occasion he feels he really couldn't be better prepared, having rehearsed his presentation from notes, run through all the support materials, put them in order the evening before and covered a range of questions and relevant answers with a colleague.

The meeting starts well until he shows the visuals. Disaster. The first slide – these were the days before PowerPoint – is upside down and out of place. The others are either back to front, inside out or on their side; everything is in the wrong order. It simply isn't possible to adjust and carry on, the presentation has to be halted, a break taken, and then the whole thing resumed.

Returning to the office in near despair, Tom discovered that after he'd finished checking the material the night before, a cleaner tidying things up on his desk had dropped the slide carousel. Not double-checking the material again before the meeting was careless. Another lesson learned: don't leave anything to chance or to anyone else, and always check everything at least twice.

Given that bad experiences are supposed to come in threes, the last presentation debacle snuck up on Tom towards the end of his first year. He'd graduated to working on another account, a piece of government business, which required presentations to be made to third parties. The whole account team was involved with developing and putting the presentation together, but Tom had been the one to actually give the presentation, while his boss performed a backstop, support role. It was a process with which Tom was now very familiar.

On the day in question, Tom had arrived back from a short break late the night before and had had no chance to rehearse or to even look at the material before heading cold into the presentation. The room was full of serious-looking men in suits and ties and hardly a smile between them. There was much rattling of cups and shuffling around before the audience settled down to listen. Putting up the first slide, Tom turned to the audience and totally forgot the opening he'd given so many times before. In fact, as the ground gave way beneath him, he'd have had difficulty remembering his own name. The silence seemed to extend into eternity.

But instead of continuing to gape at the audience he turned to the first slide, which served to remind him of the key opening points. His mouth opened and he heard himself begin the presentation: from there on in it was smooth sailing, with visuals and words all merging into a seamless whole.

In the taxi back to the agency, everyone seemed happy and his boss complimented him on his opening pause, which had certainly got the audience to pay attention! So, the learning process continued with two more important lessons. First, Tom knew to never walk into a presentation cold, however many times he might have given the presentation before. Second, he'd learned how long a pause or silence could last without it being uncomfortable for the audience. He would never be accused of not leaving enough time or air between sections and key phrases of subsequent presentations.

Coming to the end of his first year and taking stock of his achievements, Tom felt, with some justification, proud of his progress. From being the lowliest of account people, he'd become someone who'd caught the eye of the creative department and management. He'd earned the right to compete for the title of up-and-coming spirit of the agency. Central to his learning and development had been his inherent grasp of the fundamentals of spoken communications. Being able to hold the attention of his audience throughout every presentation was the result of listening, planning, timing and simplifying. And allowing for the unexpected.

The commercial world is dominated by the spoken word in all its various guises, and being a 'good' presenter is seen as one of the most powerful tools in the career-development toolbox. For those climbing the greasy pole of corporate career development, the ability to successfully handle an extraordinary general meeting, face the TV cameras in a crisis or represent the corporation's views in a takeover battle, are viewed as far more important skills than penning closely argued memos, however well written they might be. Similarly, in the public-service arena, the skills required to produce masterpieces of prose are less important than being able to verbally pitch concepts and policies.

Given that it's no longer acceptable to avoid making presentations by getting others to do them for us, is there a way that we can be sure of success? I believe there is, and that we're all capable of effective spoken communication. From the moment we learn to speak we begin to argue and make a case for ourselves; first in our families, and then in our schools, universities and work environments. If we're capable of holding a conversation then we're also capable of using those same conversational skills to construct and deliver good presentations.

Unfortunately, much of the time we've no idea why on one day we communicate really well and on the next we fail to get and hold our audience's attention. Until we're required to give regular presentations and it is pointed out to us that our performances aren't perhaps all that consistent, we haven't had to engage with thinking about what makes them successful. But there are a number of fundamental principles that, if applied, will ensure your presentations are consistently effective. I attempt to identify for you in this book what makes for effective spoken communications and how to apply that knowledge and understanding each and every time you make a presentation.

The most important key to making effective presentations is to turn them into conversations with your audience. That may sound overly simplistic, but conversation is when you are at your most effective, relaxed and understandable. Everyone struggles with their personal demons before speaking in front of an audience. But being confident that what you are planning to say and the way you are going to say it will allow you to have the impact on your audience that you want, will banish your presentation nerves and ensure that both you and your message come across at your best.

This book is designed to set out clear techniques and processes to help you build on those skills *you already possess*, while introducing you to some new ideas to help you further improve. When you reach the final page you should have no reason for disquiet about delivering presentations, because you'll have intellectually and practically engaged with the bases on which all presentations work. Nerves and stress will be something you control rather than the other way around, because you'll know their cause. Preparing your presentation will be an orderly and structured process. Delivery of your message, and the knowledge that your audience has engaged with it, will be guaranteed.

None of this is to say you won't still experience adrenalin when you make a presentation. Adrenalin is what heightens the colour and effectiveness of your delivery, but you'll now be able to use it to your advantage. Making consistently effective presentations is an art, and as with actors and musicians there are techniques and disciplines to help us overcome nerves. My aim is to ensure that you give effective presentations every time, from job interviews to crisis management. In working with the following advice and guidance you'll need to be tough on yourself in judging your own performances. Beware of easy praise, which can lull you into the belief you're doing a great job. While pushing for others to give you their honest and perhaps harsh opinion rather than settling for the comfort of instant approval, you must remain, above all, your own toughest critic.

I've divided this book into bite-size sections, and seasoned the text with advice, expertise, and anecdotes from my own experiences. These may at times seem indulgent or irrelevant, but I've included them to illustrate the points I'm making. What follows isn't a manual or a set of rules, and nor does it set out to answer every question about making presentations. What I hope to do is engage you with the intellectual and practical aspects of presenting, regardless of the audience, the location or the nature of any particular presentation. This process will provide you with a robust template for your own efforts, whatever the size or type of audience.

So, let's begin.

Summary

- Confident presenters are thin on the ground

- It's essential to combine consistency and effectiveness

- Career advancement can be enhanced with effective presentation performance

- The foundations of inconsistency are stress and adrenalin

- Conversational style is at the heart of effective communications

- Control comes from understanding how it works

- Be your own harshest critic

1:

SOME KEY PRINCIPLES

'Be yourself, everyone else is already taken.'
Oscar Wilde

Speaking objectively

What are the key objectives of any presentation? We've all sat through presentations where after a few minutes we've got no idea what the presenter's on about, and we've been shanghaied onto a voyage which has no map and apparently no final destination. If we're not clear what the presentation's about, we're unlikely to continue to give it our attention. As we saw with Tom and his interviewer, once our attention's been distracted it's virtually impossible to regain it; we've lost the thread of what's being said and are unlikely to make the effort to re-involve ourselves, however entertaining or interesting the presentation may subsequently be. Without the attention and engagement of the audience, any presentation becomes a waste of time; in fact it's even worse than that, because a presentation that loses the attention of the audience can have a negative effect on whatever cause or message we're trying to get across. Therefore, the first of the two key fundamental objectives for any presentation must be getting your message across. The second is getting your personality across.

Getting your message across

In order to get your message across effectively, you, the presenter, must gain the audience's attention and hold it for the period of the presentation. It's your personal message, not some detached, characterless script. *Remember: you're giving a presentation and not a lecture.* You want to grip the audience and they want to engage with real, live people who impress with their understanding, commitment, knowledge, sincerity and empathy. So, as a presenter, it's essential you and your personality register positively with those people listening to you.

There's a scientific theory developed by a man called Ockham, who established that we're more prone to accepting theories that are simple than those which are complicated or convoluted. *Paring down information and detail is therefore the ideal*: but being simple is not that simple. Sometimes it's possible to edit to the point where the finished presentation contains a series of unsupported assertions in the place of a logical argument.

When we attend a presentation we generally have some knowledge of the person presenting and in all probability are aware of what they're going to talk about. So it's as well to work on the basis that most presentations should concentrate on the broad brush strokes rather than focus on details which are more likely to confuse than clarify. So whatever message you wish to get across should be simple and succinct.

An old friend of mine, a keen amateur pilot, was in New York where a colleague suggested they should go along to the Pilot's Club to hear a talk by Werner von Braun. He'd been Hitler's main rocket technician, subsequently captured by US forces at the war's end and spirited away to lead the US inter-ballistic missile programme. He was to talk about the developing American space programme.

This didn't seem to be one of the more gripping invitations my friend had ever received, but he went along to fill what he thought would be an otherwise empty lunchtime. His expectations were of a dry, scientific discourse that would probably send him to sleep, and indeed the room was full of folk of a serious disposition. The audience had a smattering of younger members, but it didn't look too hopeful.

Von Braun arrived and rather than delivering an academic lecture, gave a ten-minute layman's description, accessible to all in his audience, of the programme's objectives and how they were being met, followed by a couple of clear examples of how this was being done. Not one visual aid or chart, just a 'conversation' with his audience. He then had a question-and-answer session where the technically minded could demonstrate their detailed and esoteric knowledge and the uninformed could ask about more prosaic issues. Everyone, including my friend and his colleague, felt they'd understood what the programme was all about and left the presentation feeling better informed. Above all, they felt that they *knew* Braun and that he was the right man to be in charge of such a huge and complex project. A masterly performance.

Braun could have been exclusively scientific, but that would have excluded a portion of his audience. Instead he decided to treat his audience as a group who were interested in the subject and would understand a reasonable amount of detail so long as it was couched in layman's terms. He managed to get his message across, and combined this with impressing his audience with his personality.

Get your personality across

These two overall objectives – getting your message across and getting your personality across – have to work in unison. Too much message and no personality can make any presentation a very dull thing. What do I mean by 'personality'? Well, when you listen to an effective presenter you get a sense of who they are, the language they use, and the way they impact on you. Are they forceful, quiet, sympathetic, meticulous, charismatic, understated, etc.? Each of us comes across to our audience as a particular type of person. Most importantly, we need to come across as who we really are, not what we think the audience might like or expect. Mark Twain once said, 'There are only two types of speakers in the world: 1, the nervous and 2, the liars.' A tedious presentation is very often a combination of the personality of the presenter and the way that personality has impacted on the content.

I once sat through a credentials presentation by an ad agency, thinking it was as dull as ditchwater and that the presenter was doing no favours to himself or his employer. Sometime later I had the opportunity to experience the very same presentation, given this time by a charismatic lady who made the content come alive. The result was that in the second case the agency got the chance to pitch for the business which in the first case they'd missed out on. Personality can have a very positive effect on how the message gets related to by the audience.

On the other hand, if we try to inject too much personality into the presentation, we might very well overwhelm our message. We don't want to leave a vivid impression of ourselves and no residual memory of what it was we said. We've all been overwhelmed by presenters or speakers who have projected such powerful personalities that, despite being utterly convinced by their message, five minutes after the presentation has ended we have forgotten every word they said.

For example, Clement Attlee, the prime minister who led the country in 1945, was famously dull. We recall little that he did or said, although the impact of his party's policies remains etched in history to this day. Aneurin Bevan, Attlee's Minister of Health, is remembered as a charismatic firebrand and the man who, against serious opposition from the medical profession, forced through the introduction of the National Health Service. However, while Bevan is remembered for claiming to have silenced the objections of the consultant surgeons by 'stuffing their mouths with gold', much of his message got lost in the sheer power of his delivery. It's essential to get that balance between message and personality right.

Don't let the formality get to you

The more formal the presentation, the more concerned about it we tend to become. These concerns can make us appear very different to the person our audience may know already, or know by reputation. Being faced with a hostile or disinterested audience can be daunting, but so can being faced with a room full of people you know very well. Facing friends or colleagues who have certain expectations of you and are aware of what you might consider the possible weak points in your presentation, can be tough.

The anticipation of problems raises your adrenalin levels. While this can be a useful response when trying to outrun a pursuing dog or defend against an approaching mugger, an excess of adrenalin is not that helpful if you want to impress an audience with the importance or relevance of your planned, measured and orderly presentation.

One effect of adrenalin is to speed up our performance and therefore our word-delivery. We feel the need to hurry and speak more rapidly. We're often tempted to leave the presentation track we've set down beforehand and then, showing signs of panic, our palms start to dampen, our normally acute memory departs and we feel a desire to get the whole thing over and done with as quickly as possible. The result is a rushed, incoherent and unconvincing message for the audience. Sometimes we become so affected by the stress that we miss out sections of the presentation, utterly undermining the credibility of the performance.

Every presentation should be a conversation with your audience

In most conversations we have few problems making our point, gaining support for our views or taking others along with our proposals. It's when we get to more formal occasions, with less-familiar people in less-familiar locations, that a bizarre change can take place in our characters, leaving our colleagues wondering where the confident and clear communicator has gone and who the perspiring heap of nerves might be. Stress and adrenalin are to blame, and gaining an understanding of and control over them are essential to the creation and delivery of good presentations. After all, if our behaviour seems strange to those who know us really well, imagine the impression we make on people who are less familiar with our normally competent persona. An audience can, after all, only take us at face value.

Not surprisingly, one of the commonest questions I am asked in my presentation-training sessions is how to control adrenalin and master stress. It's not at all easy to answer. Why? Because the effects of adrenalin differ according to the individual. Each of us has a different response to stressful circumstances, and finds different things stressful. Stress and the increased adrenalin it causes alert us to danger and provide us with the stimulus to get out of that danger. If you didn't experience some stress before and during a presentation it would turn out pretty dull, but equally, subsumed with stress and awash with adrenalin, you're unlikely to come across as a calm and confident presenter.

How not to come across sounding like a hamster on helium when presenting needs some pointers. First, and most important, is to accept that everyone feels nervous. Second, if you have carefully prepared and rehearsed your presentation you can feel genuine confidence in your material. On this sound basis, we can then build a similar confidence in your using the correct techniques to deliver that material. Finally, when you stand up before the audience you – and only you – know what you're going to say. So you can feel sure that as long as you use the techniques described in this book, you will have a presentation that will deliver both your message and your personality. You will be harnessing the stress rather than the stress harnessing you.

The next bad influence on our presentation can be the formality of the content or of the occasion. In our everyday environment we're comfortable talking with colleagues and those we meet socially. The language and conversational tone we use on these occasions are many miles away from those we employ when making a presentation. Lapsing into 'presentation speak', becoming stilted and mechanical the moment we stand up, might well make us sound more authoritative to our own ears, but it makes us far less credible to our audience. In fact, it's another variation on the impact of stress. It takes continued self-awareness to be able to recognize when our style and tone of delivery are going off track, leaving our normal, relaxed character behind.

Yet, very occasionally, despite all of the above pitfalls, we're struck positively with the style and effectiveness of a presenter. They've got us involved with the subject and made their key points – which we can remember! We've also gained a positive impression of their personality. These are the presentations we remember and the presenters we feel empathy towards. Imagine how much richer and better informed our lives would be if everyone worked to the same standard of effective spoken communications.

Consider how seldom colleagues pay compliments to each other for particularly well-delivered presentations and you'll be struck how such praise is the exception rather than the rule. The presenters who leave that sort of impression are those whom we feel we've been in conversation with rather than in receipt of a lecture from. They're at ease with themselves and their material and as a result we feel at ease with them. The techniques to enable you to achieve this air of being in a relaxed conversation are an important part of what I'll help you to acquire.

The central focus of your presentation should be you

One key influence in achieving effectiveness of delivery is, at the risk of sounding blindingly obvious, to make what you say interesting. Too often presentations end up being half-animated strategies that rely for interest, colour and variety on a series of overly clever visual aids. It's vital to make your words themselves interesting by grabbing the imagination of your audiences.

I was working with the credit division of an investment bank who were advising a company on floating their shares. The presentation was designed so that the proposed placement price would not be revealed until after half an hour of complex calculations and microeconomic folderol. Just before the presentation was to start, the bank's team leader announced that he'd decided to change everything around. The most important thing for the client was the revelation of that magic number. So instead of all the carefully argued bullshit justification, he went into the head client's office and told the board members the thing they'd all been wanting to hear: the proposed share price. When the presentation started, the clients were happy to sit and listen to the reasons why the price was what it was, without worrying that it would be so high that they were staring penury in the face. Meanwhile, the bank's team leader gained serious credibility.

We're inundated these days with political correctness

replacing plain English, such as BC being changed to 'Before Common Era', or 'manhole cover' becoming 'utility hole', and such worthless phrases as 'going forward' or 'at the end of the day' acting as meaningless fillers in interviews and presentations. We're regularly faced with the 'two countries divided by a common language' syndrome, with verbal misunderstandings working both ways with our American cousins. It's essential to avoid the pitfalls of these unnecessary changes to plain English that turn a simple presentation into a nightmare of wall-to-wall meaningless drivel.

You'll gain far greater engagement from an audience if you get them to use their imaginations. Giving your audience every detail, crossing every 't' and dotting every 'i', tends to exclude, and bore, them. You want your audience to reach the same conclusion as you, but how you get them to that point will be seriously helped by their participation.

When the architect of the Sydney Opera House, Jørn Utzon, was presenting his original concept to a judging committee of the city's great and good, he had to create an image for them of how the finished building would look. A model or architect's drawings weren't ever going to do the job. He had to engage them first with a *concept* that they'd be able to visualize in their own minds, despite being a group not known for their creativity. He started by asking them to imagine a line of vast sails sitting on the water in the harbour, which was an image familiar to them all. Once he'd got some of them nodding, he drew a very rough sketch of his design, by which stage everyone was nodding. He then introduced the scale model and, finally, the full architectural plans.

It's vital to get the audience to engage with whatever word-picture you choose to draw for them. Any support materials such as visual aids, props, etc., can only reinforce the message you've put across. At all stages of our progress through this book, we'll work with a number of techniques to help you do just that.

Your audience will relate to your message better if they can empathize with you

If we do indeed buy from, or listen to, those people we feel empathy towards, then what creates empathy? We judge people on the combination of how they look and what they say. Almost before a presenter starts to speak, the audience will have formed an emotional rather than a rational view of the person in front of them: 'Do I feel comfortable with, or disinclined to listen to, this person?' As I've said, the most effective communicators are those with whom we feel we're having a chat rather than those who lecture at us. We're at our most convincing when we're relaxed and conversational. So, to repeat, as close to conversational as possible is the best presentational mode, *but it's vital to take on board that conversational doesn't work the same way as presentational.*

So how does conversation work?

This isn't quite the dumb question you might at first think. Because conversation is such a wired-in function, we don't generally give its workings or ground rules too much consideration. Conversation is fragmented rather than orderly and sequential, and most importantly, *it's full of interaction.* You say something, then you allow time for it to register, and wait for a sign of approval or understanding through verbal response as well as facial movements, at which point you respond accordingly.

If a man is standing on a cliff with a megaphone, shouting out to a crew of a boat that they're heading for some rocks just below, he might well think that he's communicated with the boat. However it's not until the boat has changed course to avoid the rocks that *effective* communication has taken place. This is a simple example of how communications is *receiver*-driven, a two-way process of *stimulus and response*.

There are going to be those occasions in a conversation when it's clear that you haven't totally got your message across and so have to go back over it in order to ensure that your point has been properly communicated. Once you've received the signal that your co-conversationalist has got the point, then – and only then – you can move on, knowing they are still with you. To disallow them that courtesy is to effectively exclude them from involvement in anything more you have to say. You dismiss them from the conversation.

When looked at via video replay, it becomes clear that conversation doesn't follow the cut-and-dried nature of normal, formalized 'presentationese'. Go ahead, get hold of a camera and record yourself and other people in a free-ranging conversation. You'll be surprised at how disorderly it all is. We would, of course, shy away from constructing a presentation, even an informal one, in such a way.

Here's an example of how people actually speak:

'Morning.'
'Lovely day . . . well, I don't mean lovely, more, well

you know, actually, it'd be great to have the sun again, because it cheers me up so much.'

'Yeah, I couldn't agree more . . . it's been far too long . . . or maybe not far too long, more . . . no, you're right, it's great . . . although did you see the paper this morning on sunburn?'

And so on, moving with careless ease from subject to subject, starting from a single-word greeting. But always in response to what the other person has said.

In conversation we indulge in a lot of mind-changing, non-sequiturs, interruptions and speaking over others, often ending up back where we started. But that's how we talk, generally in an effort to ensure we've communicated as effectively as we can. Again, observe friends and colleagues.

Therefore, when you're putting together your presentation you need to consider how you can add some order and structure to this less-than-orderly form. If you made a presentation an exact replica of a conversation, your audience would be bemused: you need to help them through the process. To ensure that those two key objectives of personality *and* message have consistently been met, you need to come across as 'yourself' within a disciplined framework.

Summary

- **The aim is to get your message, and your personality, across to the audience**

- **Formality of occasion leads to stress and anxiety, which in turn affect delivery**

- Presentations are based on conversations – beware 'presentationese'

- The focus of the presentation should be you – it must be interesting, using colourful language and examples

- Your audience relate better to someone they empathize with – informality in conversational style is the key

- Conversation is fragmented, ungrammatical, involving signs of approval and repetition to confirm understanding between speaker and receiver

2:

HOW TO ACHIEVE CONSISTENCY

*'There is nothing constant in this world
but inconsistency.'*
Jonathan Swift

We've established how you can, in principle, minimize the problems of adrenalin and stress at the same time as ensuring that you express yourself in a clear, everyday, conversational style. This might seem something of a daunting task, but there are some simple and fundamental techniques you can call upon to help.

A familiar example of the problem

Let's consider a high-profile event covered by the media: the Queen's speech, delivered from the throne at the state opening of Parliament. Had our much-admired and -loved monarch been trained in the art of giving a good presentation, she would not read her script. Her dependence on the words on the page makes for a reliable but dull performance. In order to grab our attention, speakers need to do something more.

How often have we been to conferences, seminars and grand occasions where the speakers, often known to us by

their stellar reputations, have failed utterly to engage us the audience, leaving us with a far less favourable impression of their capabilities than before they opened their mouths? Frances Rodman had it pretty right when she said: 'The problem with speeches isn't so much knowing when to stop, as knowing when not to begin.'

Why do many speakers and presenters come across as wooden and unconvincing, despite having the benefit of autocue and all the other bells and whistles of modern high-tech communications? Is there some surprisingly simple answer to these performance problems? I believe there is.

The importance of time

There's a common theme running through the problems outlined above: time. The speaker doesn't allow the audience enough time to absorb the message. Remember the importance of the conversational style? As I pointed out earlier, spoken communication is a two-way process, and the speaker can't simply aim endless, undifferentiated sentences at the audience. Audiences can only take in the information they're being given in the way it's delivered. The required joining of a willing and effective speaker with a willing and attentive audience can only come about in cases where the speaker respects the audience and allows them time to absorb the message. Engagement with the audience has to be earned by showing due consideration; if no consideration is shown, the audience will tune out and not bother to tune back in. Once lost, an audience is virtually impossible to regain. Author and public speaking consultant Lilly Walters maintained that 'the success of your presentation will be judged not by the knowledge you send but by what the listener receives.'

It's your audience who drive the pace of your presentation. Ignore that truth at your peril. Remember, it's not all about you. It's a whole lot more about the people you're talking to, although unfortunately we don't always see things as they are, rather we tend to see them as *we* are, only concerned for how we sound rather than how the audience hear us. Without the willing engagement of your audience, you might as well be talking to an empty room. You must consider not only the ability of the audience to relate to what you're saying, but their ability to absorb your message at the speed you're delivering it.

An attendee at a spoken communications course I was running said he hoped I could help him with the construction and delivery of his presentation because he'd got so much he wanted to say. I asked him if he'd considered whether his audience might not want to hear absolutely everything he'd prepared. He ignored my observation and the discipline it might impose on him. When he gave the first run-through of his presentation he'd still tried to cram in the enormous number of facts he believed he had to get across. He hadn't allowed himself time to draw breath during the process, let alone given his audience the time to engage with him. His presentation ended up being wall-to-wall words, with absolutely no differentiation between the importance of each element of his subject matter. It was entirely transmitter rather than receiver-driven.

This appalling first attempt left me and his fellow course attendees gasping for breath and completely disengaged. Why? Because there was no space for us to take in one message and, having done so, move on to the next point he wanted to make. It was a single, *entirely unpunctuated* stream of consciousness.

In spoken communications, punctuation is communicated by *a pause* to allow your audience the time to keep up with what you're saying and then continue to follow what you say next. In comparison, if there is no punctuation or proper sentence construction in a book, just an impenetrable mass of words, we similarly disengage. It's essential to take on board the need for punctuation and then construct your presentation accordingly. However elegant your prose and argument, or well-designed your visual aids, if your audience haven't followed you at the pace you've set, then all is unfortunately for nought. You must set a pace at which the audience can follow what you have to say, which is why I'm insisting that effective spoken communications are receiver-driven.

Holding your audience

How, in a darkened auditorium, can you know that your audience haven't nodded off the moment you've got past your introduction? Be reassured, it's perfectly possible to be certain they're hanging on your every word, but only if you've been delivering your speech or presentation effectively. This means moving at a measured pace, allowing your audience the time to continue to be engaged with your message. Don't worry, there'll be audible signs of engagement: laughter at the right moments, attentive silence as opposed to shuffling of papers or feet or other such noises. Even in the dark you should be able to sense the audience's basic reactions: you'll instinctively know. If you're taking account of their speed of absorption rather than your speed of delivery, have no fear, they'll stay with you. If you're in a well-lit conference room, which is ideally where you should be, and are able to see the whites of your audience's eyes, you'll be able to see very quickly whether they're hanging on your every word, or just hanging around till the coffee arrives.

The means to do it

Think back to how people sound and behave in conversation. There's a theory about how communications work, from the basic to the electronic forms. A unit of transferable information is defined as a 'bit', and conversations, in their most absorbable form, are broken up into 'bits' or bite-sized chunks. What do I mean by a 'bit'? Again, it will vary from individual to individual. Some of us are able to pick off the page large chunks of words: it has something to do with peripheral vision. However, unless it's a short sentence, it's unlikely we'll be able to pick up the whole thing at once. Rather it's what you can remember between glancing down at the page and looking up again, and this might be two or three words or a whole phrase. This is generally why we tend to work from notes or bullet points when putting together our presentations, although, as we'll cover later, working from a pre-prepared script may, from time to time, be a necessity. *All presentations are compressions of information.*

The right type of information-compression?

Think back again to how people sound and behave in conversation. We all speak in 'bites' of information and we all give nonverbal signs of assent and understanding when we're ready to move on, or have agreed with a point being made. These are not always elegantly formed or logically ordered and can at times seem disjointed.

We regularly restate material when we feel an audience hasn't quite grasped what we've said. If the message hasn't registered, there's no point in moving on, because the audience will feel disregarded and tune out. In conversations, were you able to replay them, you'd be surprised by the length of the pauses left between thoughts, often to the point where in retrospect they seem exaggerated. However, few people complain that they've been given *too much time* to absorb messages; they're more likely to notice when the time they're given is too little.

Is there a way to replicate or match this conversational style when delivering a presentation? Yes, there is, but it'll take some determined application on your part to absorb, engage, experiment and eventually feel comfortable with the technique. So I'm going to ask you to be patient while I explain and then get you to experiment. There are always those who grasp this idea quickly, but there are many who initially find that it doesn't sit happily with the presentational style they've developed and feel comfortable with. Interestingly, it's these people who, once they've persevered, often gain the most.

A proposed methodology

Sir Ralph Richardson once said that 'the most precious things in speeches are the pauses'. Mark Twain agreed: 'The right word may be effective, but no word was ever as effective as a rightly timed pause.'* This is also the case in presentations. The art of pausing is built into all actors' training. Watch a TV drama or a film and note how there are significant silences to let particular lines or phrases sink into the audience. Similarly, news readers or announcers on TV or radio allow significant pauses to punctuate the various stories they're reporting. The question of how a particular stage technique can possibly help you appear more natural

---

* Ron Powers, *Dangerous Water: A Biography of the Boy Who Became Mark Twain* (Da Capo Press, 1999), p. 174

and conversational in giving a presentation does need further explanation. Below is a speech made by Napoleon to his Old Guard before his departure for Elba, which I have marked-up to show how to make the most of the pausing technique.

> Soldiers of my Old Guard. _Pause_ I bid you farewell. _Pause_ For twenty years I have constantly accompanied you on the road to honour _Pause_ and glory _Pause_. In these latter times, as in the days of our prosperity _Pause_ you _Pause_ have invariably been models of courage and fidelity. _Pause_ With men such as you _Pause_ our cause could not be lost, _Pause_ but the war would have been interminable, _Pause_ it would have been civil war _Pause_ and that would have entailed deeper misfortunes on France. _Pause_ I have sacrificed all of my interests to those of the country. _Pause_ I go _Pause_ but you _Pause_ my friends _Pause_ will continue to serve France. _Pause_ Her happiness was my only thought. _Pause_ It will still be the object of my wishes. _Pause_ Do not regret my fate. _Pause_ If I have consented to survive, it is to serve your glory. _Pause_ I intend to write the history _Pause_ of the great achievements we have performed together. _Pause_ Adieu, my friends. _Pause_ Would I could press you all to my heart.
>
> – Napoleon Bonaparte, 20 April 1814

There wasn't a dry eye in the house. Without the pauses, some of which are longer than others for even greater effect, the speech would not be dramatic; in fact it would be rather bland.

Remember, we're trying to overcome the effects of stress and adrenalin and, by the timing of our delivery, to give our audience the chance to absorb our message.

You'll be surprised by how much more natural you'll sound if you adopt the following as a key basic presentational discipline, working with the pausing technique used by actors and the occasional defeated dictator.

What I'm going to propose will at first seem strange and need considerable practice before you'll see the full benefits. The process is best entered into with an unfamiliar set-text speech, as well as a presentation from your own material, but one you've not made too recently. Speeches and texts are readily available from the internet. I suggest that you search 'chamber of commerce speeches' and there should be a considerable range of unexciting but useable texts available. Once you download a speech or two, before printing them off make sure they are in 14-point Times New Roman font and double-spaced, which makes them far more easy to read. You'll also need someone to observe and comment on your performance, as well as a camera with which you can film yourself so that you can review your performance afterwards.

Step 1

Record yourself and your observer in conversation. It doesn't really matter what you talk about, but it must be a two-way conversation and last for, say, three to four minutes at least. You need to be able to reach a point where you're talking in a natural conversational manner and not concerned about the camera running. Next, take the material you've chosen to use from one of your previous presentations and deliver three to four minutes to camera, without any rehearsal. This will give a petty reliable impression of how you sound and look to your audience on the average day. You might well be surprised at how flat your performance is.

Step 2

Take whatever set text you've selected and deliver it to the camera and your observer, with no rehearsal. Don't deliver the whole thing; just, say, another three to four minutes and then stop. This will give you an idea of how, under more than the average amount of stress, you can often appear to your audience when giving presentations from a script; not unlike the Queen!

Step 3

Using the same set-text material and recording yourself as before, with someone to point out where you fall short on the technique below, perform the following sequence:

1. Start off by first looking at your audience.

2. Then look down and pick up a 'bite' of words – as many as you can pick up in a quick glance. There's no prize for memorizing more than you can pick up in that quick glance.

3. Next, look up at your audience/camera and take a *noticeable* pause before you say whatever phrase you've just picked up off the page. *Don't worry that you've only picked up very few words*. And don't attempt to add anything to make the individual bite sound any more sensible.

4. Then, take another *noticeable* pause.

5. Finally, look down again and start the process once more from the beginning.

6. Repeat until you get a sequence completely correct – however long or frustrating a process that might prove to be.

Get the above sequence well established before you start to record yourself . . .

To repeat:

1. Look at audience

2. Look down and pick up a bite of words

3. Look up and pause

4. Say the words

5. Pause again

6. Look down and continue to repeat

Step 4

Now, with the benefit of having successfully taken on board the 'drill', take your own material from a previous presentation and, in light of what you've learned from your personal recording, deliver three to four minutes of it to camera using the technique you've just acquired. You will now have two versions of your previous presentation, the version similar to your average performance and the version where you have built in the 'drill'.

Step 5

Compare and contrast the two versions of the presentation. There should be a marked improvement in terms of colour, tone, personality, and audience perception of content and theme, in your performance with the 'drill'. Yes, it certainly won't make you look entirely natural, but the overall impression should be one of improvement.

You won't find this whole exercise as simple as it might sound. In fact, I've known some people find it extremely difficult to achieve a satisfactory series of recordings. Generally it is the second pause that's most difficult to hold, as your natural inclination when your mind is empty is to refer back to the script. Remember: *both pauses have to be long enough to make them clearly noticeable*, and they will, to begin with, probably make you feel uncomfortable. However, if you force yourself to practise until you get it absolutely right, and if you have someone to help you, when you have it established in your mind, the technique will stick and you will see why it has the effect it does.

It's essential that you use both first and second pauses.

Why? The first pause you take is your 'consideration' pause. A thinking pause that allows you sufficient space to order your thoughts and to inject meaning and focus into what you're saying. The mind does work surprisingly quickly if you let it. It will have compressed what you can comfortably pick up in a glance. Saying those few words you've picked up in a 'bite' isn't dissimilar to the way we speak in conversation, i.e. not necessarily strictly grammatical, and coming often in short phrases and 'bites'. Once you've said the phrase, the second pause is the 'got it?' pause, to ensure you allow your audience enough time to absorb whatever information you've just given to them.

Two pauses. Verbal punctuation to give injections of time and space into what you're saying. If the pauses aren't long enough, it can seem to your audience as though you're dismissing them from the point and are moving on, regardless of whether they've taken it in or not. It's essential you persevere with the practising until you've built the pauses into your delivery to the satisfaction of your observer.

Now it is time to review all the material you've recorded up to this point. Your review should take the form of watching the recording of yourself and your observer in conversation: note the fragmented, disjointed and ungrammatical nature of everyday conversation. Then review the sequence in which you give the presentation without preparation. Finally, review the sequence in which you deliver the presentation with the 'pausing' technique. Note the difference between yourself at high speed without preparation, and when you allow your audience sufficient time to absorb what you have to say.

Do I expect you to adopt this bizarre straightjacket every time you make a presentation? No, I most certainly do not! But I do want you to engage your intellect and consider what the demonstration illustrates.

The theory is that when we treat our presentations as entirely different from our everyday conversational style and delivery, they're dull and colourless. When we replicate, albeit somewhat exaggeratedly, what happens in everyday conversation, the effectiveness of the communication is considerably improved. We need to make our presentations as close to that conversational style of delivery as we can, because we need to make ourselves as much as possible the relaxed person that others know us to be from their experience of us in everyday conversation.

Okay, so now you know how to ensure your audience will engage with you and then stay with your presentation.

You now have to ensure that the *content* of the presentation lives up to your delivery. Let's move on.

Summary

- Try to avoid reading set texts: cf the Queen's speech

- The importance of time; presentations are two-way between speaker and receiver; the necessity of verbal punctuation

- Keeping the audience's attention; measured pace; consideration for the audience; 'consideration' pause; 'got it?' pause

- Presentations are compressions of ideas and words, done in real time

- Right type of compression; bits and bites, absorbable chunks of information

- Use acting technique for time and space; create with 'drill'; step by step to effective pausing and verbal punctuation. *NB: This technique must be used with care and rehearsal.*

3:

HOW TO CONSTRUCT YOUR PRESENTATION

'Half the world is composed of people who have something to say and can't, while the other half have nothing to say and keep on saying it.'
Robert Frost

Preparation and strategy

Take the planning seriously

Tony Blair famously banged on about the importance of 'education, education, education'. With regard to making presentations, we should, before ever thinking of the end product, dedicate ourselves to 'preparation, preparation, preparation'. We've all been either the victims of our own inadequate preparation, or suffered at the hands of someone who forgot about its importance. My guess is that, albeit probably with an unhappy shiver of recall, we can all remember the time when, on the way to the meeting, we tried to put down our ideas in preparation for a quick informal presentation. Why didn't we do it earlier? Dashing down some impromptu thoughts on the back of an envelope, we then proceeded to get torn to shreds by our well-informed and hostile audience, who are all too quickly aware of the poverty of our preparation. What about those times when, with toe-curling embarrassment, you sat through some poorly prepared presenter's attempt to wing it, while all you wanted to do was make a break for freedom and fresh air through the exit door?

To stand up before an audience without having prepared properly is to put yourself at the gravest risk of delivering a presentation that fails. It doesn't have to be that way. Bill Shankley, a legendary football manager, said that winning games wasn't a matter of life and death, it was much more important than that. Presentations have to be approached from the same perspective. After all, what's the point of giving a presentation when you yourself aren't convinced of the strength and relevance of your argument, or that you're the best person to make the case?

1. Get your planning started early

We've all been guilty of thinking that the simplest and quickest way to construct our presentation is to start from the visual aids. Once they've been sorted out, the presentation pretty much writes itself, doesn't it? They'll provide the framework to base everything on, won't they? These are easy mistakes to make, and ones I'll be addressing in detail in the later chapter on visual aids. Many of us spend years making regular presentations, often at short notice, ranging from low-importance to very high-profile events. With such a varied range of possible occasions and content, maintaining the same level of dedication to preparation and effective delivery can prove difficult. Remember what happened to Tom, in the story I told in the Introduction? It is vital to approach *each and every* presentation as of equal importance, as either a career-enhancing or a career-inhibiting opportunity.

There's no substitute for proper planning, which always has to start with the objectives of the presentation from the perspective of your audience as well as yourself. What are you trying to achieve with your presentation, what are the main points of focus and what do you want your audience to take away from your presentation when you finish speaking? If you can't clearly identify these requirements and believe they're achievable, then it's very possible your presentation will not engage your audience and will be ineffective.

As an example of setting clear and achievable objectives, an ad agency I worked with recently on a new-business pitch set their objectives initially as *a*) win the business they were pitching for from a multinational, multi-brand confectionery manufacturer, by being assigned at least two of the company's major brands; *b*) achieve a fee equivalent to 15 per cent of the advertising spend; and *c*) convince the company to run the advertising concepts presented for the brands unchanged.

My advice to the pitch team was that they were setting objectives that could well prove difficult to achieve, and that their failure to achieve them might well be unavoidable. Certain failure is never an attractive objective or outcome. We agreed they should adjust their objectives to gaining an assignment of at least one brand, achieving agreement to a minimum fee equivalent to 10 per cent of ad spend, and getting agreement to research at least two of the concepts presented. These objectives also allowed for some wriggle room for negotiation up or down, depending on how the wind appeared to be blowing. Following their pitch, the agency were thrilled to achieve the revised objectives, whereas they'd have regarded themselves as failing badly had they set the bar unreasonably high and not achieved the unachievable. It's essential to set objectives, but equally essential to ensure they are realistically achievable.

The next step is to identify the most effective strategy to ensure your audience's engagement with, as well as approval and endorsement of, your proposals. What are the key points or facts that underpin the flow and argument contained in your presentation? Get your objectives clear and the logic-flow of your arguments mapped out. In the majority of cases, presentations are most effective when based on factual rather than emotional information. Something that an audience can get its teeth into. Even the effective selling of creative concepts is generally based on logical arguments.

The flow of any presentation has to be consecutive and logical so that the argument hangs together seamlessly. This won't happen unless you've identified, and linked, the key points of your argument. Finding out midway that two key planks of your argument don't effectively combine can destroy the credibility of your whole presentation. Once the flow and logic have been worked out, then you must ensure you've sufficient detail in the body of your presentation to support and carry through your argument.

2. Nothing beats practice

Having created the argument and flow of the presentation, the structure of the argument, and the supporting evidence for your case, you then have to ensure that this potentially immaculate piece of spoken communications succeeds in its aims. But even before determining whether your presentation works, it would be sensible to have some sort of template against which to judge your efforts. That template should include:

1. Opening remarks: set the scene, ease the audience into the presentation. No waffle, but related to a central theme that binds the presentation and objectives together.

2. Key objectives: what, specifically, do you want your audience to do as a result of listening to the presentation.

3. Create a theme for the presentation: an idea that will bind all the elements of the presentation together.

4. Identify strategic issues: the skeleton around which your argument will be built.

5. Create the presentation argument-flow: the flesh on the skeleton, with detailed support to dovetail with the strategic issues and objectives.

6. Summary and conclusions: tell them what you told them at the start. Reprise the theme.

7. Timing: check that you haven't exceeded twenty to thirty minutes max, confirming with a rehearsal.

Once you've complied with the template, one rehearsal with an observer should be sufficient to tighten the final presentation. However, what may have appeared to you to be a seamless work of verbal genius may have some inherent problems. The time to discover that the logic-flow doesn't quite work and there are gaps in the general flow of the presentation isn't in front of your eventual live audience. That's why at least one formal rehearsal is an essential quality check.

How to refine your presentation structure

1. Scope

Your presentation shouldn't try to achieve too much. Your audience will just about be able to take on board three key facts or fundamental points with their associated support arguments. Sad but true, I'm afraid. If you try to throw everything into the presentation, you'll end up with an impenetrable laundry list and your audience will rapidly tune out. The spoken-communications course attendee I mentioned earlier was advised to limit himself to the three most important elements of his presentation and focus on these as the essential points he wished his audience to take away. Ignoring the advice and packing his presentation with less-than-vital information simply made it more difficult to absorb, which in turn resulted in an inability to understand and then a rejection of the whole message by the audience.

Don't overreach yourself with either the scope or the content.

2. How long is too long?

The question of length is another issue that causes debate. There's been a considerable amount of research into what should constitute an ideal length for a presentation. After all this learned consideration, with consultants furrowing their brows and academics sucking their teeth, the conclusion reached was that as a general rule, forty minutes is the optimum length. Given that forty minutes is the length of a school lesson, perhaps there's something to be said for that conclusion, and maybe our concentration span has been habituated to this time length. My own experience has been that twenty to thirty minutes is sufficient for most presentations in most situations. We ignore the fundamental advice to limit duration at our peril, as the following example illustrates.

A major international technology corporation brought its European regional managers together every quarter to make presentations on major developments in their markets. Each manager would arrive with competitive quantities of visual aids, spending ever-increasing amounts of time praising their particular achievements.

These meetings inevitably began to expand in hours and cost, to the point where the European managing director thought it would be sensible to research the outcome. Phoning each of the regional managers, a month after the last meeting, it was discovered they remembered absolutely nothing from the time spent watching all the presentations . . . except what they themselves had presented personally. When the same research was repeated after the next meeting, this time only a week later, the results were exactly the same. Any further meetings were cancelled immediately and a substantial contribution was made to the bottom line of the European division. For our own purposes, there's only one conclusion to draw:

Keep it simple, short, and to the point. The brain will only absorb what the bum can stand!

3. Theme

As discussed above, every presentation benefits from a unifying theme which is regularly referred to. Your theme will provide a thread to tie all the parts of the presentation together, enabling the audience to follow you through to the end. Without this central theme, your presentation can end up feeling rudderless and lacking in focus.

For instance, in the 1970s British Airways used the theme throughout their marketing and advertising of 'We'll take more care of you'. Apart from being a 'soft' proposition, it was lamentably untrue, as research showed that on service/care, BA fell far short of its rivals. However, it did fly more people to and from more destinations than any other airline. This made it possible to say that it was 'the world's favourite airline'. The presentation by the new agency to win the business centred on this theme of preference, rather than service. At each stage the argument was brought back to the theme of 'the world's favourite airline' and the step-change this proposition would create in the airline's marketing, image and operations. A decade of change and success followed.

A theme helps keep your audience on track, and its repetition keeps them focussed.

4. Delivery method

You must decide early on in the preparation what your chosen method of delivery is going to be. To some degree this may depend on the location and audience. For instance, if you're presenting to 200 people from a podium in a conference centre, you're likely to be legislated by the conference organizer into speaking from a set script in order to ensure a well-ordered and time-limited programme. Whereas if you're speaking to a small internal meeting you could well choose to speak from notes or bullet-point prompts. Also, you have to decide early in the process whether you want to use visual aids and, if so, what form they'll take. I'm going to cover the different delivery formats, such as script, notes and off-the-cuff, and the use of visual aids, in detail later.

The right delivery method for the right venue will help get the right response.

How to refine your presentation content

1. Key messages

Returning to the three-or-so key messages you can realistically expect your audience to take in: nothing beats repetition. The old-but-relevant piece of advice that you should tell them, tell them again, and finally tell them one more time for luck still holds true. In the words of Winston Churchill: 'If you have an important point to make, don't try to be subtle or clever. Use a pile driver. Hit the point once. Then come back and hit it again. Then hit it a third time – a tremendous whack!'

Repetition really does help to drive home a well-prepared presentation. If you are to effectively communicate with, and control, your audience you must regularly emphasize what you consider to be the most important parts of your message.

Keep your key messages simple and clear and regularly repeat them.

2. Main content

Once you've identified what you absolutely have to get across to your audience, you'll also have created the structure of the presentation and its outcome. The support for those key points should then fall into place for the lines of your argument as well as the theme that summarizes them.

As an illustration of this, the marketing department of a bank had to present a new contactless credit card to a credit committee. The card had three key points. It was to be: 1) easily obtained; 2) better-distributed, with more points of potential use than any other card on the market; 3) able to offer a higher credit limit than competitors. For each of these three points the department had to create a series of support proofs. This automatically divided the presentation into three sections which then had to be effectively linked to provide a seamless argument. With a strong introduction, in which they established their theme, the team then moved on to the key points and their linked arguments, using everyday illustrations. They finished with a summary of what they'd argued. During the presentation they made their key points, made them again and finally made them one more time. The credit committee were convinced, not by any means an easy task with such an extremely conservative bunch. The card was launched successfully.

In putting together the overall presentation you must remember to give it a beginning, a middle and an end. This may sound obvious, but if your audience don't have a clear idea of how long they're expected to pay attention they're more than likely to zone out. In the case of the credit-card presentation, this meant identifying how long the presentation should be, pointing up a well-constructed three-point argument and then making it clear when the argument moved from one point to another, and finally making a clear summary.

Create signposts for your audience and then make sure you stick to the track.

3. Use of examples

Remember that if your presentation is on a complex or technical subject, it may be helpful to offer a simplified image or example. Examples and analogies bring a subject to life by illuminating and clarifying.

Here's an example of how examples make a difference. I worked with the sales engineers of Boeing, whose job was to deal with airline general managements regarding specification technicalities and detailed measurements, making for rather exclusive language and presentations that didn't often engage their audiences. Concentration on all the technical stuff meant their presentations ended up being, quite frankly, dull. Discussion of the thickness of the aircraft fuselage became an abstruse and complex matter of microns and materials. The engineers were finding it difficult to keep the airline executives they dealt with interested and awake.

When I pushed them to find an example to illustrate what they were trying to say, one engineer came up with the notion of using the thickness of a Coke can as the illustration of the thickness of the aircraft fuselage, which brought the whole matter down to earth without too much of a bump. The truth is that even the most technical boffins are

also human beings who have families, read the paper, and deal in the everyday; just like the rest of us.

Make it easy for your audience, keep the language and examples as everyday and simple as possible.

4. Personal style and tone

With the rise of advisers and consultants in the arena of making presentations, there's been a good deal of talk about the use of psychology, body language, dressing for success and other influences on the quality of presentations, over and above the content and delivery. It's tempting to believe there are a range of supplementary skills and tricks that can positively affect our performance, without which, however dedicated our efforts, we probably won't cut the mustard as presenters.

Before entering this particular arena, it's worth remembering that all of us have some degree of social sensibility and have been successful in our chosen careers. I suggest that this is due to being able, amongst other things, to read the intentions of people and gain their cooperation. If you're able to engage with and use the sort of advice given in this book, then the darker arts of personal presentation can be put to one side until you reach the point where your skills have become so developed that subjective additions such as how you dress, your control of body language, etc. might possibly give you a further marginal advantage or refinement in your presentation technique. In the meantime, however, we're talking about more basic common-sense concepts combined with some self-awareness.

Beware the temptation towards overcomplication or dubiously subjective refinements.

5. Humour: an added dimension or a risk?

The other area to be approached with caution is the use of humour. I'm sure that most of us have suffered that excruciating moment when the presenter makes a misguided attempt at either a humorous start or finish, to be met with stony silence from the audience. It's a serious risk to assume that what might appear amusing and witty to you and a couple of colleagues, even in rehearsal, is going to be taken the same way by your audience in the cold and unkind light of a presentation at 8.30 a.m. on a frosty February morning.

When humour works it can be an effective aid to communications, engaging the audience at a fundamental level. There are those who are naturally funny and can boost their presentations with enviable wit. However, there are also those to whom wit and humour are distant strangers, in which case their attempted use can be a disaster. Before you decide to employ your natural humour, make a very careful assessment of what you really mean to achieve, and whether it will be either relevant or amusing to your audience. If the answer to these questions is even a maybe, drop the jokes.

Stick to getting the basics right before deciding to reveal your particular sense of humour.

6. A strong start as well as a strong finish

It's remarkable how often, when we go to presentations, the whole affair gets off to a rocky start even without any unsuccessful attempts at being funny. It's a certainty that if you don't successfully engage your audience's attention at the very beginning of your presentation, you won't succeed in your key objectives. If your audience is not with you right from the start, you're never going to get them to switch on to what you're saying halfway through. You have to nail them from the first word, remembering that those first few seconds are when you win or lose an audience's involvement. Then you must keep them engaged until clearly letting them know when you've finally finished.

In one of my group sessions, a bank executive working in a particularly pedestrian part of the business, when doing the first run-through of her presentation, had sent all of us to sleep within minutes – almost before the presentation had started, in fact. When we discussed the problems with her presentation in the group, she was adamant that both presentation and subject matter had to be very straightforward because of the seriousness of her area of responsibility: the compliance function in the credit department of her bank. The poor woman also found her job deeply unmotivating, so struggled to make it sound even vaguely interesting.

At the end of the first day I insisted that, overnight, she rework the presentation and concentrate on getting off to a strong, engaging start. Then the next day we could judge how much she'd improved the impact of her presentation. Despite having taken on board the rest of my advice, she was still unconvinced she'd be able to make a presentation on her role in compliance even minimally engaging. However, off she went, shaking her head in what looked like despair. The following morning she was first up to present, having – I hoped – incorporated the improvements we'd requested she work on overnight.

She opened her presentation by asking us to imagine entering a building in the City, the HQ of a major investment bank, to hear a presentation from the compliance department. Taking a lift to the thirtieth floor we arrive at the plushest of boardrooms, with a stunning view over the

cityscape. The windows are open, with the curtains blowing into the room. There's no one in the room and there's an eerie silence save for the whistling wind and the curtains rustling. Avoiding the temptation of the coffee and chocolate digestives on the boardroom table, we approach the window, and are confronted with two sets of white knuckles belonging to a now-regretful attempted suicide, who is hanging on for dear life to the window sill. Although we try to grab the person's arms and drag them back into the room, it is all too little too late, and the poor unfortunate plummets to the pavement below, letting out an eerie scream.

My unwilling compliance officer gave a long pause before concluding that there, sadly, perished the banker who had chosen not to listen to the compliance department when he'd been told about the regulatory problems with his derivative scheme. She then proceeded, for the rest of her presentation, to use as her theme the 'saviour' role of her department and

how it could help bankers avoid the fate of the poor unfortunate owner of the knuckles on the window sill. Even early on a chilly, foggy winter's morning there was absolutely no doubt she'd got our attention.

You've only got a few seconds to convince your audience they should bother to listen to you.

7. Avoiding distractions

When you've only got a few moments at the beginning of a presentation to grab the audience's attention, introducing yourself and telling them what you're going to talk about is a waste of your and their time. By being in the room they've committed themselves to listen to you; they probably already know who you are and what you're going to talk to them about. Try to avoid, if at all possible, the opening visual aid of a slide with your name, rank and the 'title' of your presentation, which I'll cover in more detail later. While this talking about yourself might make *you* feel more comfortable, it does nothing for your audience. They've come to listen to what you've got to say and you'd be well advised to get on with it without too much delay. Someone, of course, might have come to the wrong room, but that doesn't happen too frequently, in my experience.

While there will always be habitual latecomers, there's certainly no need to make allowances for them by inconveniencing or distracting those in your audience who've had the good manners to arrive on time. Breaking the well-designed thread of your presentation only serves to support the bad manners of people who think their time is more valuable than yours or that of the rest of your audience. Leave them to solve the problem they've caused for themselves, either by staying at the back of the room, or by causing further unpopular interruption by trying to find an available seat. In the event of the latecomer being your chairman or managing director, however, it might wise to make an exception to this particular rule and find them a seat at the front!

In smaller internal meetings, where coffee or refreshments are served, ensure you don't have to battle with the clatter of cups and pre-meeting chatter that hasn't yet died down. Give your audience time, let them settle; you aren't required to put yourself at an immediate disadvantage by allowing some of your audience to divert everyone's attention from you.

As you progress through your presentation, and you've clearly identified the signposts on the track down which you're leading your audience, reaching a clear conclusion is as important as getting off to an impactful start. We've all

sat there at the end of a presentation wondering whether it's actually ended or not. Having followed the maxim of 'tell 'em, tell 'em again, and then tell 'em one more time', remember what was said earlier about creating an engaging theme for your presentation. If you've created a central theme, it will have provided an effective thread as the presentation progresses and give you the basis on which to construct an effective and impactful conclusion. The BA illustration provides a good example of this. Having started off by saying that the presentation would identify why service wasn't the differentiating factor and preference was, it was possible to refer back to the theme as the natural conclusion.

If your presentation doesn't start well it's very unlikely to end well.

8. Visual aids and their influence

At this point I'm going to touch on the subject of visual aids (VAs) but will return to them in more detail later. Once you've created your presentation and are satisfied with the flow and content, having identified clearly the main points as discussed above, it's time to look at what visual aids can contribute to *reinforcing* the argument you've created. Unfortunately, all too often visual aids are used like a drunk uses a lamppost, more for support than for illumination.

In order to do a specific job – without distracting your audience's attention from you the presenter – your VAs must highlight and reiterate points you've made, *and not become the script for you to read from.* Always ensure that you have a rehearsal which includes your VAs, in order to ensure they're actually doing what you want them to do, and doing it in the right place in your presentation.

Stick to VAs that reinforce your key messages.

Summary

- Get the strategy right

- Beware the dangers of lack of preparation: don't wing it

- Get your planning started early; every presentation is important; sort out objectives and strategy first, then detail and support

- The importance of rehearsal; does the presentation work?; logic-flow; options for review and revision

- Refine the presentation structure

- Scope; three key facts; too much makes audience tune out

- Ideal length forty minutes at most, twenty to thirty ideal; keep it simple and short

- Theme-centralizing idea binds the elements

- Key messages: define and repeat regularly with theme

- Main content: theme and key messages are the structure to fill in around; give audience route map

- Examples: use everyday ones in everyday language

- Personal style: be yourself, don't worry about peripherals, complications or refinements

- Humour: don't attempt it, unless you're a famous stand-up!

- Strong start and finish; you have a few seconds; don't waffle to opening slide; tell them when you've finished

- Avoid distractions; allow the audience to settle; use the theme as your focus

4:

HOW TO DELIVER YOUR PRESENTATION

'It usually takes me more than three weeks
to prepare a good impromptu speech.'
Mark Twain

Ensuring the most effective delivery

1. The rehearsal

You've gone through all the stages, adopting all the disciplines mentioned above, and you've now got what you believe to be the perfectly formed presentation. But there's a strong possibility that it might not be quite as perfectly formed as you believe. What sounds to you like seamless logic might not sound the same way to your audience. The most common issue is that of linkage, or the gaps between the sections of which every presentation is formed. When moving from one section to the next, there is quite often a discernible hiatus. These potholes are easy enough to fill if you have at least one rehearsal.

Too many rehearsals, however, can be almost as bad as none at all. To deliver a fresh and presentation requires us to inject enthusiasm and energy into our delivery. This is less possible if we've ground through the process four or five times over the previous two days. One run-through should be sufficient to enable you to build in any correc-tions, amendments or additions. Your rehearsal should always be in front of an audience, even if it's only one person, and delivered in full with any VAs, etc. that you intend to use. This will point up any of those gaps we discussed earlier, and ensure that the totality of the presentation is subjected to objective scrutiny before being launched on a live audience.

Don't assume everything will work fine – always test it out first.

2. Timing

However flattered you are to have received an invitation to speak to an august body of your peers for two hours – always answer with a polite no. Two hours is far too long. No matter how much new and exciting information you might have, it simply couldn't take two hours to impart. *Remember: the job of a presentation is to compress, précis, summarize and package an argument or information.* It's all about precision, not duration.

Thinking back to your school days, and the standard forty-minute lesson, do you remember those double lessons, especially on your least favourite subjects, where you spent most of the second half of the eighty minutes looking out the window?

If you're rigorous in your judgement of your own material, I believe that, in the vast majority of presen-tations, you'll be able to make considerable cuts at the rehearsal stage, without affecting the flow and logic of what you have to say. Of course, this advice will depend on your subject and material. While you should always aim to create a presentation of around forty minutes maximum, adherence to this time-frame has to be tempered by circumstance.

However, it's essential to rigorously limit the length of your presentation to allow your audience to absorb all of your message. Interrogate every word to ensure that it contributes to the overall argument and end result. If it doesn't, cut it out. *Your presentation will almost certainly be more effective at half its initial length.* No audience will take offence if you say you're going to take forty minutes but then only take twenty (although this might, of course, scupper the schedule!).

While what you say and how you say it may be most important to you, how long you take may be more important to your audience. As Lord Reading once said, 'Always be shorter than anybody dared to hope.'

3. Sticking to the script

Having followed the advice above about preparing a finely tuned and tightly timed presentation, you proceed to the lectern. All goes well until halfway through, when you're seized by a blinding flash of inspiration which you feel compelled to share with your unsuspecting audience. Until this point, they've been hanging on your every word and giving regular signs of total engagement. As you proceed to impart your inspired addition, you sense them shifting in their seats; somehow or other you've lost them. Maybe your addition wasn't quite as intriguing as you'd thought? Maybe the audience sensed you'd headed off on a verbal wild goose chase? You've become a victim of the '. . . and another thing . . .' pitfall, and you've got to get both your audience and yourself back on track.

Discovering a brilliant or killer point, and then expressing it, while in the middle of a presentation is an indulgence to be avoided at all costs. Should such a temptation present itself to you, ignore it and carry on with your script or notes as they stand. If any idea is that good, you'd have thought of it before rather than during the presentation, wouldn't you? And besides, the middle of your presentation is no time to discover the hidden depths of your creativity. The risk of derailing your presentation and not achieving one or both of your two key objectives is simply too great.

In the event that at the end of your presentation proper you still feel that new spark of genius to be burning brightly, there's always the possibility of adding an addendum or perhaps referring to the idea in the question-and-answer session. Giving in to the temptation to deviate from your script is rather like being on a journey where time is tight and deciding just for the hell of it to take a detour down what looks like an interesting side road. You're heading off into the unknown with no idea how you're going to get back on track and arrive at your agreed destination at the agreed

time. You run the risk, by adding to your rehearsed and timed presentation, of going seriously over time, a crime your audience is unlikely to forgive.

Avoid the temptation to vary from what you know works well. Remind yourself it all worked well at rehearsal.

4. Setup and location

All too often the actual location of the presentation is the last thing anyone considers. Despite sophisticated audio-visual setups, custom-built auditoriums and the rest of the paraphernalia of the modern communications industry, it's remarkable how often the location for a presentation is less than ideal.

A successful US advertising agency, Needham Harper & Steers, refused point-blank to make any presentation to a potential client until they'd had the chance to inspect the proposed location at least twenty-four hours beforehand. On more than one occasion this policy either resulted in the prospective client withdrawing the invitation to make the presentation, or the agency itself withdrawing. Whichever of these alternatives occurred, the agency avoided putting themselves in a location which, they believed, would negatively affect the reception of their work.

Ensure you control the field of battle as well as the timing of the conflict.

5. Be a stickler for detail

While you might consider this level of preoccupation with detail obsessive and not always possible or advisable, it's nevertheless important to ensure that the facilities and location for your presentation are up to what you require and that all the equipment works. Even in your own premises, there are often bad meeting rooms that can be changed and facilities that should be double-checked.

We've all been in the situation where the equipment, for instance, is technically unsuitable, doesn't relate to your material in some way or other, has different hardware suppliers, or non-matching leads, etc. To tell a story against myself: having attempted, unsuccessfully, to check out a venue where I was running a course, I finally accepted I'd have to chance it and trust that the venue would sort out any technical issues with slide and video display. They didn't, and so while it took an age to find a technician to resolve an issue with a video camera, a dozen people had to sit there and wait. You're never too old or supposedly experienced to learn. There's absolutely no merit to be gained in discovering problems five minutes before the start of your presentation. At the very least, well ahead of the start time, find a technician and run through the visual aids. It's also important to do a sound check.

Finally, unless it's absolutely unavoidable – and generally it never is – don't present in a room in which the stage is poorly lit. Inevitably the audience will give their attention to whatever is most visible and that won't be you, especially if you're stuck in a half-lit corner. Their attention will naturally go to whatever VAs you put up on the screen, or the messages pinging in on their iPhones. There is a very entertaining but acutely performed video on YouTube by the late, great Alan Rickman about this very issue, called *Disastrous Presentation*, which is well worth looking at. The focus of the presentation must be you. It's surprising how often, even in today's more savvy communication culture, presentations are handled in an inexplicably amateur fashion.

Don't leave anything to chance, or to anyone else, and ensure that you're always seen – literally – in the best light.

Summary

- Importance of rehearsing: seamless-logic check; beware linkage; repetition causes staleness

- Timing: don't try the audience's patience; stick to ideal length; summarize don't extend; edit harshly; length is key audience concern

- Stick to the script: don't overrun; no flashes of inspiration; no 'and another thing . . .'

- Setup and location: choose your own location; check out anyone else's; insist on what you need

- Detail: check out rooms; double-check equipment; stage lighting; ensure you're properly lit.

5:

HOW TO ENSURE THAT YOU SAY WHAT YOU WANT TO SAY IN THE WAY YOU WANT TO SAY IT

*'Much speech is one thing,
well-timed speech is another'*
Sophocles

Selecting and refining the best delivery method

Set text/script

1. The advanced version

If you're presenting in a large, formal situation such as at a large conference, where it's essential to stick to timing, then giving a speech from a fully pre-written, timed text is advisable. This is probably the format we dread the most because, as already discussed, simply reciting a speech doesn't lend it credibility and it seldom if ever sounds spontaneous. Unfortunately, we don't have the wherewithal to deliver such a formal text other than by reading it and even using the 'bits' technique we covered earlier, it would probably be difficult . . . or would it? We've already discussed the possibility of using the pausing technique to replicate everyday conversation more closely. If you are comfortable with that method, I'm about to illustrate an advanced technique which will help you, in the particular case of formal set-text presentations, appear even more natural and make your presentation seem as if it's being delivered from the heart rather than straight off the page.

This technique entails extending the period during which you're looking down at the speech on the page and delivering part of a sentence until you reach a point where you can look up and finish that sentence, using a 'got it?' pause as a point of emphasis. It gives a generally smoother effect and when viewed by the audience, appears both natural and confident. Below is what I call the 'bathtub diagram' which illustrates how the technique works.

As I hope you can see, this method smooths the ups and downs of the basic technique to avoid any tendency towards

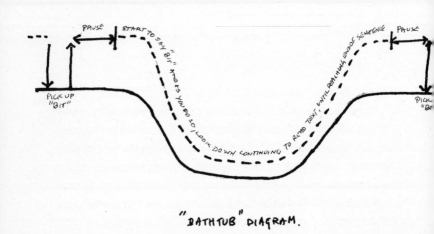

"BATHTUB" DIAGRAM.

short, staccato delivery. If you add this refinement to your already established pattern of pausing, it'll ensure a particularly effective delivery of any formal set script or text. The most important thing to remember when delivering any set-text speech is to maintain those two pauses to ensure effective punctuation of what would otherwise become a tedious litany.

Over the length of a set-text presentation, sticking religiously to the two pauses would make you come across as something of an automaton: not an ideal result. So the refinement described above will ensure a more relaxed and normal delivery, while still allowing you to punctuate your presentation effectively. It's going to take a fair bit of rehearsal – *once more with a camera and a critical observer* – to get the technique to become a comfortable part of your presentation repertoire, but it's well worth persevering with for those cases where set-text presentations are a regular requirement.

If you're comfortable with your material, the audience will be too.

2. To autocue or not?

In a set-text presentation, there's always the possibility of using an autocue. This technique has upsides and downsides. It's a format that does require some familiarity, as it moves at the pace of the speaker, speeding up or slowing down depending on the delivery. This can have the unfortunate effect of the speaker gathering pace, for whatever reason, and the autocue consequently gathering pace; the speaker then starts to speak even faster to keep up and so on. Such a performance doesn't tend to lend credibility to any presentation.

There was a Conservative Party conference where it had been decided that everyone, without exception, was to use autocue. However, there were some speakers who weren't totally comfortable, or hadn't practised enough, with the technique. Time pressures ensured the autocue had to be persevered with regardless, despite the fact that there'd been some dreadful mishaps at the rehearsal. The result, for one unfortunate senior minister, was that he and the machine slowed down to the point where the audience began to wonder if the speaker was suffering from an illness of some sort. As he was the Health Secretary, this proved particularly galling.

Autocue isn't the automatic answer.

3. Choosing the set-text option should now be easier

So the use of a prepared text has potential pitfalls and we've all been subjected to presentations that have come a cropper. However, there will inevitably be situations where the right format, indeed the only format, is a prepared text.

In such instances, making sure that all the advice above has been reviewed and proper rehearsal time ensured will minimize any problems caused by unfamiliarity.

Always ensure you select the most suitable format for the particular occasion.

Notes and headings

1. A familiar thing?

We've now arrived at the presentation format we're most familiar and comfortable with – one where we can rely on our own notes. Notes are the delivery method most suited to the majority of smaller presentation situations. Unfortunately, they're also the delivery method most prone to abuse through carelessness or laziness. Because our presentation notes are written in our own personal code, we tend not to interrogate them as harshly as perhaps we should. After all, it's us presenting, we created the notes, we know what we want to say: so everything will be fine . . . won't it? Built into this attitude lies the potential for disaster. Individual eccentricities are perfectly acceptable in conversation, but when you're creating notes to see you through the intricacies of an argument during a half-hour presentation before a potentially hostile audience, you need to ensure you've left absolutely nothing to chance.

Familiarity mustn't be allowed to breed contempt.

2. A very personal thing

If you were to ask four people to show you their notes for the same presentation, those notes would vary dramatically.

Notes are intensely personal to the presenter. If you were to lend your notes to a colleague to present on your behalf, they'd generally find them impossible to work from.

There are various schools of thought about what format one's notes should adopt, which is why we often see people at the beginning of presentations either shuffling what appears to be a pack of cards or gaily waving what might be a replica of Neville Chamberlain's famous Munich speech. It's never reassuring to see presenters struggling to physically control their material.

The selection of the most effective format is a matter for the individual. Some people create very foreshortened notes, to the extent where they are no more than bullet-point stimuli. Others need longer and more detailed input. But whatever else you may or may not include, the notes that work for you must contain reference to and stimulation for *all you want to say*. Without some additional stimulus, most of us find it generally impossible to remember supplementary facts and information while in the process of making a presentation. If it needs saying then your notes should refer to it, and if it's not in your notes then it probably doesn't need saying.

Even though you wrote those notes, make sure they're full enough to do the job.

3. What's the ideal length?

I'm frequently asked the question 'what length should my notes be?' The guidance I offer is that, in principle, if your presentation is thirty minutes long, then you should have somewhere in the region of three pages of handwritten notes, allowing for approximately ten minutes of presentation per page. Also remember that what is perfectly readable to you when you make your handwritten notes may be less so when you're standing up before an audience. If you go much over the above length, you'll end up with what is not far off a prepared text. If you go for a shorter length, you might well find yourself unwittingly running out of stimulus for things you really want to say. Experimentation with what is the right length in your particular case is essential, and you'll soon find your own particular comfort level. There's certainly no hard-and-fast rule, but it's surprising how often, when you time your presentation, it works out to be very close to one page of notes being equal to ten minutes of presentation.

Nor is there a hard-and-fast rule for what should or should not go into your notes, and in what form. The inclusion of complete sentences, buzz-phrases or even bullet points is dependent on what works for you: there's no one-size-fits-all format. I'm sure you'll get to recognize the stimuli that best generate what you want to say and how you want to say it. Finally, a rehearsal ensures that your notes actually are sufficient, effective and readable.

Ideal notes are as much about comfort and confidence as they are about timing and content.

4. A dependable route map

Effective notes should provide you with a reliable route map for your presentation to follow. In other words, your notes should make specific reference to what you want to say, with headings to point out your key communication points and cues for any visual aids clearly marked. It's like a comparison between an Ordnance Survey map and a Google print-off; the former is an absolute detailed guide, while the latter may get you there but sometimes be a bit too broad-brushstroke and therefore a risky guide. A risk you don't need to take.

Everything you need to point you in the right direction should be in your notes, *and nothing else*. The headings of each section will mark out your progress through the key points, and each subsection note should contain the nub of what you need to say, supplemented where necessary with further points to back up the main flow of the presentation.

This is where you might consider including any bright, *but scripted*, 'spontaneous' asides, so they don't interrupt the thrust of your presentation, while still seeming to be of the moment.

Because you're familiar with your subject don't be tempted to indulge in any showing-off by including stuff to impress rather than to advance your argument. If you do so, you may well notice that the notes become over-extended and wordy, in which case it's time to wield the red pen. Such indulgence is obvious to your audience and rather than acting as an integral part of your route map, it simply serves to distract or confuse.

Once you've decided on the elements of the presentation, stick to them.

5. Ensuring a seamless flow

You need to ensure your notes contain sufficient stimulus to include every key element in the presentation, in the right order and with the right emphasis. You should include in your notes those places where you want to use a pause as a serious piece of punctuation, and where you want to move on from one key point to another. With a clear demarcation provided by effective pauses, both you and your audience will get a sense of movement and flow. If you have an organized presentation, your audience will sense that and keep with you, confident that you aren't about to lead them into uncharted waters.

Make sure your notes contain everything you're going to talk about, and refer to whatever is necessary to make for effective communication.

6. A game of cards?

Note cards are often preferred because they're less conspicuous than sheets of paper. However, cards can and quite often do get muddled up in the nervous shuffling of material during presentations. Once muddled, any hope of a smooth and seamless presentation has been lost. Reorganizing a number of cards in mid presentation, while keeping an audience engaged, is a task nobody would willingly undertake.

Sheets of handwritten notes, and much-amended sheets of paper, can be difficult to handle and offer just as many opportunities to undermine your presentation. Typed sheets have to be in a readable type size and should be double-spaced to allow for marks of emphasis or additions to be included. Whichever format is chosen, you must ensure your notes provide you with all the stimulus you need. I should re-emphasize that every individual has their preferred format and style of notes and if you're pressured into changing from your preference, don't give way unless you feel it will benefit you to do so.

Use the note format that is most comfortable for you – take your own advice and stick with your choice.

7. The PowerPoint trap

A dangerous habit has sprung up with the advent of reliance on computer-led presentation aids such as PowerPoint. Because printouts of the slides, with any notes included on

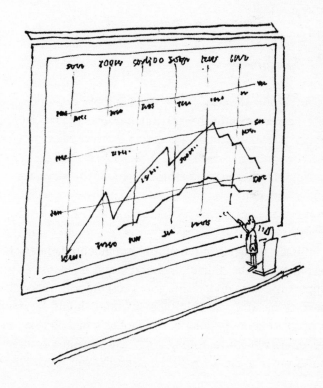

the side of each sheet, are all too readily available, it's now common to see presenters using these slide printouts as their presentation notes. This tends to put the visual aids at the front and centre of the presentation. Everything we've talked about so far has focussed on ensuring that you, the presenter, are the centre of attention for your audience and that you and your message are inextricably linked. If you use slides as your notes you *will* end up talking to the slides and distracting attention from yourself. Rather than the slides supporting and underpinning what you've said, they will become the key focus of the presentation.

Slides can't talk. You have to do the talking to engage your audience.

Summary

- **The importance of maintaining those two key pauses to ensure effective punctuation**

- **Autocue isn't the automatic answer**

- **Select the most suitable format for the particular occasion**

- **Notes should provide you with a route map**

- **If it needs saying then your notes should refer to it**

- **Beware using slides as your notes, and distracting attention from yourself**

6:

HOW TO HANDLE QUESTION-AND-ANSWER SESSIONS

'The wise man doesn't give the right answers,
he poses the right questions.'
Claude Levi-Strauss

Treading carefully

We've now reached the point where you've created and delivered a pretty near perfect presentation. Generally, it will be followed by a question-and-answer session, which, as I'm sure you've already experienced, can be a two-edged sword. On the one hand it offers the opportunity to demonstrate your personality in free form, away from the straightjacket of a presentation. On the other, it's an opportunity to undo whatever good work you might have just accomplished with your effective presentation.

The relief that comes from having finished a presentation can cause an unfortunate relaxation in concentration. Answered in the wrong way, due to this relaxation, an apparently harmless question can offer up any number of hostages to fortune. The temptation to show off your superior knowledge can be overwhelming. It's as well to remember that a Q&A session is not an opportunity to put your feet up; it has the potential to be something of a snake pit. Similarly, a successful presentation followed by an invitation to discuss it further over lunch, or any other dangerously relaxed situation, can, without care, lead to some unguarded remark that undoes all your previous good work. A simple piece of advice is to avoid staying for lunch or drinks if at all possible: always plead another appointment and take the opportunity to quit while you're ahead.

The end of the presentation doesn't mean you can relax.

Listening is a vital skill

Remember: *the Q&A session is just as much receiver-driven as the main part of your presentation*. You are now expected to *listen as well as talk*, and listening, because it's acquired in silence, is an often much-underrated skill. How many times have you observed a presenter start to answer before the questioner has finished? All right, I hear you say, how often does some idiot questioner ramble on and on without getting to the point? That may be the case, but unfortunately interrupting or cutting off such a questioner won't help you achieve your aim of positively establishing your personality with your audience.

Further: how annoying do you find it when politicians and others on a discussion panel speak over and interrupt each other, and how often do you conclude that the participants are simply not listening? This judgement doesn't add anything to your view of their personality. The requirements of the Q&A session are no different to those of your main presentation. You must allow your audience time to ask their questions, you must be seen to think about the answer and you must then allow the audience time to have absorbed and understood your response. All this is to aid the audience's establishment of a positive view of your personality.

It's possible to identify the exact point where a presenter stops listening to your question because they've made up their mind as to their answer. It's the point where you can see their gaze move away from you and their lips start to move: check it out, it really is noticeable. This happens because they've moved from 'listening' to 'transmission mode'. By doing this, there's a risk of their not properly catching the whole question and as a result giving an irrelevant, incomplete or incorrect answer: potentially dangerous and certainly useless.

Ignoring part of a question is dangerous because the part you've missed, either by design or default, might well be where the real focus of the question lies. In that case, how do you come across to the audience? Certainly as someone who isn't listening, possibly someone trying to evade the question, and definitely someone who hasn't considered the needs of their audience.

If, however, a proper and satisfactory answer has been given to a question, then it's feasible to close down any further questioning by saying the subject has been covered sufficiently and move on by asking if there are others in the audience with questions they'd like to ask.

There's no point in being a good presenter if you aren't prepared to listen.

Take care not to over-answer

Just as there are overcomplicated and tricky questions, so there are overcomplicated and verbose answers. This can sometimes be the result of not listening. If a question is not listened to, the result will inevitably be that it's not properly responded to. The presenter disengages from the questioner, then picks up they're not satisfied with the answer. Panicking that there's a problem, the presenter then tends to add the first thing that comes to mind, to fill the questioning silence. This makes a tricky situation far worse. A very clear case of talking when one should be thinking: a tendency that causes an awful lot of problems in Q&A sessions.

A desire to show off our superior knowledge is another temptation to be avoided. Just because we happen to know something vaguely connected to the question, which we believe to be a fascinating insight, doesn't mean our audience will feel the same. Attempting to include too many elements in an answer can often be confusing, even if, from your perspective, you think you're giving a more complete answer. Generally, the best answer is a short answer, or certainly one that only answers the question you've been asked. You can always ask the questioner whether or not you've satisfactorily covered the question, and if you get a quizzical look, ask them to follow up on your answer. A supplementary question can then be answered properly and succinctly.

Controlling tricky questioners can be a challenge. Silence can be used effectively in such a circumstance by leaving a long pause after they've finished asking the question. The questioner often views this as an opportunity to add a bit extra or to ramble on even further, undermining the integrity of their original question and allowing you to select the most telling part to answer. Leaving a long pause after you've finished answering clearly punctuates the exchange and shows you've nothing more to say on that particular subject. This tactic also discourages the questioner from reviving a discussion which you clearly view as over.

One thing is certain, there are always going to be dumb questions and dumb questioners. It's not difficult to show how verbally proficient you are at the expense of a questioner, but that won't always endear you to the rest of your audience.

If you give yourself a 'consideration' pause before delivering your response, you'll allow yourself time to tone down any answer that may verge on the aggressive. Also, there's no problem in finding yourself saying one thing, realizing it'll give the wrong impression and changing tack in mid answer. As we've already seen, that's exactly what we do in conversation, where we deem it necessary. It's also a clear sign that you're not just rolling out a set of pat answers, but are looking to positively engage with your audience and their concerns.

For some of us, sarcasm is a tool that comes all too readily to hand. It has no place in presentations or Q&A sessions. It never comes across well and I'm sure we can all recall the moment when an impressive speaker has destroyed their hard-won credibility by resorting to sarcasm to put down a troublesome questioner.

Remember, you're trying to win the audience over, not defeat them. You have the means of keeping control; use silence as an ally.

Don't rush to answer

There's no prize for a speedy answer, only potential problems from answering too quickly. Give yourself sufficient time to clarify your thoughts and deliver an effective and convincing response. This allows you to retain the initiative rather than ceding it to any difficult characters in your audience.

When you've been asked the question, don't leap into an immediate answer. Give yourself that serious 'consideration' pause. Regardless of how erudite your response might be, it does no harm at all to be seen to have thought about what you have to say before speaking. Once you've given the answer, give your questioner a serious 'got it?' pause. If you immediately look away, you dismiss the questioner, which will appear inconsiderate as well as undermining any positive impact your answer might have given. Always ask if you've satisfactorily answered the question from the questioner's perspective, before moving on.

Giving yourself time helps you to order, refine and shape your thoughts. This 'air' around your answer, as well as proving you don't have a pre-packaged response immediately to hand, shows you to be both thoughtful and confident.

Answer in haste, regret at leisure.

If you don't know, admit it

The worst thing you can do in a Q&A session is to offer up hostages to fortune. Quite often audience members turn out to be better informed than you on matters of particular detail. Asserting something you aren't certain about is high-risk. Once you begin to try to talk your way out of trouble, you can often dig yourself into an even deeper hole. The questioner who's found your weak spot knows enough, in all probability, to continue to pin you to the lectern.

In the event of not knowing the answer, simply admit the fact: how disarming is that? A subsequent offer to get back to the questioner with the answer they're looking for is one option which will sit well with the rest of the audience. If you allow a good, long 'got it?' pause after the offer, only a vindictive questioner would come back for another attempt at taking a chunk out of you. This ensures that the audience will have complete sympathy with your situation and your openness and probably feel out of sympathy with an aggressive questioner, who'll sense it and pull his horns in.

Getting trapped is far worse than coming clean.

Handling the persistent questioner

This problem tends to be found in the media arena, where interviewers can refuse to accept that you don't have a definitive answer. However, it can happen in any Q&A session where a questioner isn't going to be put off until getting the answer they believe they're entitled to.

Saying, after your first attempt, that you've answered the question and are going to move on to the next questioner is one strategy. However, this response could be seen as dismissive. In certain circumstances it's possible to plead commercial security, copyright or privacy, but that has to be a fact and not a ruse subsequently proved to be untrue.

Another technique is to offer the opportunity of a conversation at the end of the Q&A session, rather than continuing at length with a line of questioning the audience might well be finding of limited interest.

The important thing, in the face of a persistent questioner or a persistent line of questioning from a number of questioners, is to stick to your original position. Once you've committed yourself to a position, it's unwise to change horses in midstream, however attractive that might seem. But having said that, if it's clear that you've been discovered in an untenable position, come clean. I'm going to cover both media interviews and crisis-management techniques later.

Be determined, but avoid being determined to be wrong.

The long and involved question

There's a questioner in every audience who, either unable to use one word where twenty will do, or through malicious intent, will ask a question that ends up taking longer than your answer, even vying with your presentation for length. Two minutes into such a question, neither you nor the other audience members have a clue what it's actually about. This is one reason why you should always have a pen and some paper on you. This will enable you to jot down the elements of a complicated or convoluted question and play them back for confirmation by the questioner. This also allows you to rephrase or reorder what's clearly a trick question intended to cause you problems.

It's also true that the person asking the long and involved question is often someone who likes the sound of their own voice and the thought of impressing their fellow audience members. The temptation is to be dismissive or perhaps to register visible signs of fatigue during the question. While some of your audience might be in sympathy with your frustration, many will sympathize with the poor questioner who you've just cut down to size when all they wanted was a straight answer. Of course, it's a matter for your judgement as to how to handle such audience members, but it's certainly worth having thought through the possibilities and options of any Q&A session before you volunteer to face the challenge.

They may be tedious, but long and involved questions deserve equal consideration.

Calling it a day

The temptation to allow too much time for too many questions must be avoided. Remember, for those in the audience who don't ask questions, this part of your presentation might prove dull, however lively your answers. You'd be well advised before starting the Q&A session to announce how long it will last and stick to that limitation. Five minutes is generally ample time. You can always offer an extension, once you're certain that the questions aren't heading off in the wrong direction. The length of your answers is also an area where you should err on the side of brevity. Remember, the questioner can always ask a supplementary question.

Don't entangle yourself by allowing your audience too much rope.

Speaking off the cuff

You're at a meeting where you're suddenly asked to make a few opening, or indeed closing, remarks: a perfect opportunity to blow your credibility. The problem with speaking off the cuff is that you can either do it or you can't. It's not a skill that can be taught. If you're not a natural off-the-cuff operator, you need to think carefully about how to manage these situations. The natural speaker, nine times out of ten, will appear confident and as a result will control the situation. The less natural speaker will, to a similar degree, appear unsure, under-briefed, and will fail to control the situation. In which case it's better to say nothing, or to defer any comments to a future point, either immediately after the Q&A or even to a different time or place, where you'll be in a more controllable situation.

The best strategy is to minimize what you have to say. It's safer to simply give a brief welcome or a polite 'thank you for coming'. Remember: there's no such thing as really and truly speaking off the cuff. The very best impromptu speeches are the ones written well in advance. Those individuals capable of *appearing* to act in an impromptu fashion turn out, pretty much without exception, to have made some preparation beforehand. They have mentally logged the areas they might need to talk about and noted the sort of responses they're likely to give; even to the point of making some bullet-point notes.

Is there a difference between answering questions and speaking off the cuff? Absolutely: however unsatisfactory your answer in a Q&A session, it's a particular response to a specific question, whereas off-the-cuff remarks don't necessarily have any anchoring relationship with what's gone before. They can land you in completely uncharted waters. Many a person has lived to regret their off-the-cuff moments.

There was an infamous case not too long ago where the eponymous owner of Ratners, the major retail jeweller, completely unprompted, announced in the presence of the press that his company's products were 'crap'. This off-the-cuff remark resulted not only in his own sidelining, but also in a considerable hit on the market capitalization of the firm. Not to mention a very hard row to hoe for the company's PR agency!

You can never be *forced* to answer a question, reply to an overly aggressive challenge, or speak when you're unprepared. Two particular situations where it's essential to remember this observation are crisis management and media interviews, both of which I cover as the final subject area in this book.

No one can force you to say anything – it has to be your decision, so tread carefully!

Summary

- Tread carefully in Q&A; don't relax concentration; no question is harmless; don't overstay your welcome

- Listening is a vital skill; presentations are *receiver-driven*; don't interrupt questions; presentations and Q&A require same disciplines

- Don't over-answer; no 'and another thing . . .'; give clear short answers; take a 'consideration' pause before answering; don't flaunt superior knowledge; finish each question with a 'got it?' pause

- Don't rush to answer; good 'consideration' pause; audience need to see you thinking; ensure quality of answer

- Avoid sarcasm and aggression; dumb questions and questioners; tolerance versus disdain; audience must be willingly on your side

- Admit you don't know; no hostages to fortune; offer post-session conversation; don't get trapped

- Persistent questioners? Accept follow-ups; stick to your guns; agree to disagree; offer of more info

- Calling it a day: everyone not interested in Q&A; too much Q&A undermines positives; stick to agreed timing

- Long, involved questions: pen and paper; split question into sections; repeat question back; select what to answer; give due consideration

- Speaking off the cuff – avoid if at all possible; don't lose continuity; uncharted territory; prepare; no one can force you to say anything

7:

HOW TO MAKE VISUAL AIDS WORK FOR YOU

'Sometimes one picture is equal to 30 pages of discourse, just as there are things images are completely incapable of communicating.'
William S. Burroughs

The development of visual aids

Not so long ago, visual aids were a fairly uncomplicated story. A slide or two was the norm for illustrating a complex set of figures or a remote, unfamiliar location. Today they are a much thornier area. There has been an explosion of graphic-support programmes such as Prezl, Keynote, Slide Rocket, Google and of course PowerPoint. You can now have the full range of bells and whistles – sound, movement and an array of typefaces, etc. There is no end to the audio-visual world you can create, but the question you must ask yourself is: should I? Without, I hope, sounding like too much of a Luddite, it's worth considering some of the concerns that visual aids can raise.

We've seen that every presentation involves the never-easy struggle to get your message across to your audience.

So let's consider what might distract them from concentrating on *you*. A particular visual aid might punch home a key point, but in doing so might also prevent your audience from reacting positively to your personality. Is the visual aid going to *reinforce* your message, or be the message itself? It's essential that you interrogate each and every visual aid to ensure that it is doing a *specific job* and not interfering with the prime objectives of message- *and* personality-communication.

In preparing your presentation, it's all too easy to start from the wrong end. By this I mean that you might construct your presentation from a series of headings, which you then build into slides, which you use as prompts or notes for the actual presentation. This method has a number of pitfalls. First, the tendency is to think that the VAs alone are sufficient to drive the presentation forward; that they can give the required stimulus. This is not necessarily the case. Suddenly, in mid presentation, the slide might fail to provide you with the link you wish to make with your next point.

Second, by using the slide as an aide-memoire you will need to have put it up *before* you reach the point it's required to illustrate. So either you have to leave the audience to read the slide before you start talking, or you find yourself talking while they're trying to read the slide. Either way, neither you nor the slide are getting the audience's maximum concentration.

Third and most important, once the audience realizes all you're doing is paraphrasing your slides, they're going to make a choice to either read the slides themselves or to listen to you. In which case, either you or your slides are redundant. If they've opted to read the slides, your objective of communicating your personality has been completely surrendered.

This issue, which I touched on earlier, is compounded by the availability of computer programmes which have notes alongside the slide references on your computer screen. These are all very well and good, but may make the process of delivering the presentation more demanding than necessary, with the notes being either over-complex or too small to read, or both. Keeping all elements of the presentation simple and manageable is the safest and most sensible course. There is also the possibility of printing off the slides and any notes you have made alongside them. With rehearsal input and the inevitable last-minute changes of mind revisions get made to the notes but not necessarily to the slides themselves, which could have serious potential for confusion and disruption to your presentation delivery. If you keep the slides and your notes separate, you'll ensure there's no potential for any dissonance between what's in front of you and what you put up as a slide.

The strategic arguments for making sure your visual aids aid your presentation with visual support – as the name suggests – are therefore clear. The nub of the matter is that they are there to *support* you, not be a substitute for you. They should be a reinforcement of your key points *after* you've made them, not during, and not before. They aren't your script, your aide-memoire, or your notes. *You* are the centre of the action.

The audience are there to see and listen to you, not to look at your slides.

Is there a preferred type of slide?

Yes: as short and as simple as possible. Long, complicated, wordy slides are bad slides. There has been considerable research done on how many words there should be on a single slide, and while the results vary, the range of variation is between six and ten. Your audience generally won't read long wordy slides and if they attempt to do so, you're allowing their attention to be diverted. To attempt to get around this shorter-is-better requirement, there's a temptation to use 'build-up' slides to avoid one wordy slide, where you start with one point and on consecutive slides add another point. However, you end up with a wordy slide in the end anyway, as well as an even more bored audience! This is also a bad idea because you're still depending on the slides as the mechanic to get your point across, with the attendant risk of marginalizing yourself.

There's also the temptation to add extra interest or energy to your presentation by inserting 'entertaining' elements to your slides, such as movement, dissolves, changing typefaces, etc. This is to be strenuously resisted, as it'll distract rather than focus your audience's attention. In principle, it's best for your slides to be bullet-point summaries of what you have told your audience, nailing your key points and reinforcing your message.

An important technical point to remember is to have a blank screen between each visual aid. This ensures the focus is on you while you're talking, with no chance for the audience to be idly wondering why there is a misspelling, or why you've chosen that particular background colour or typeface. Your audience's attention doesn't need any encouragement to wander.

Short, simple slides are the best.

The lighter the room the better

It isn't rocket science to make the point that if you're speaking from notes in a darkened room they can be somewhat difficult to read. The temptation therefore is again to use your VAs as your script, with the problems I've already mentioned. Where you're speaking to a larger auditorium audience there's of course the possibility you'll be at a lectern, with back-projected slides. In this event, make sure the conference organizers light you properly. Also, the audience need to see you to gain an impression of your personality: are they likely to accept the message of a disembodied voice in the dark?

Every presenter should be afraid of the dark.

VAs are there to support your illumination

Why do most presenters start by introducing themselves, with a slide of their name, title, company, etc? Because it allows them to ease their way into the presentation with a line or two they can't fluff. However, this meets neither of the key objectives and runs the risk of making the presenter appear unconfident. The VAs should act as summary points to reiterate what you've said: remember the 'tell 'em, tell 'em again, and then tell 'em one last time' advice earlier. It's all too easy to fall into the trap of seeing the slides as the interesting part of the presentation, while you're just there to press the forward button.

VAs aren't there to entertain or vamp up the presenter, they're there to support.

Technology deceives more than it flatters

Technology has the scary ability to break down at the most inappropriate times. It should be possible for you to give your presentation without any VAs at all, as would be the case in the event of a failure of the technology for displaying your material, as for instance with a power failure.

When McDonald's decided, some decades ago, to hold their first international conference in London, someone managed to forget that there was a difference between the US and Europe. At the rehearsal stage it became evident that various technical functions of the pulsed slide presentations of all the delegates wouldn't work because of the difference between 240 and 110 volts electricity supply, and would have to be totally re-jigged. Even the introduction of a transformer didn't help, as the pulse-tape programming was too sensitive to accept the change in current. An illustration of unintended consequences, and technology letting you down. And a perfect illustration of the merits of a rehearsal.

Beware reliance upon complicated, new or untried technology.

Who should leave the most lasting impression – the presenter or their VAs?

It is the best presenters rather than their slides that stick in our memories. I've never heard anyone leaving a presentation saying they were mightily impressed with the VAs or with a particular typeface or, for that matter, with how wonderful the computer graphics were. But I've heard them asking who the presenter was.

On the other hand I do remember presentations given by Eurotunnel, where they regularly used one particular slide of a diagram illustrating the relative difference in time and distance between two places to illustrate a point about journey times. It resembled a distorted fried egg and every time it made an appearance in a presentation, the audience all thought of fried eggs. Once their imaginations had been kidnapped by the weirdness of the VA, they switched off from the content of the presentation. To add to the unintended consequences of the visual side of things, each speaker had been issued with an electronic laser pointer, to indicate the salient points on each VA to the audience. Unfortunately all these lasers did was to accentuate any minor hand movements, which made the pointers leap around all over the screen like demented spiders. A fatal combination of poor VA, technical intrusion, and the fact that these presentations were made in the dark, guaranteed failed communications.

Always identify clearly what each and every VA is supposed to achieve.

Summary

- Slides aren't your script; concentrate on you; reinforce points with slide

- Preferred VAs: short and simple; beware too much information; no 'build-ups'; no clever graphics; keep it simple

- Keep it light: dark room = concentration on slide not you; formal occasion needs proper lighting; communicating personality difficult in the dark

- VAs support your illumination: you're the focus

- Technology can deceive: breakdown problems;

equipment compatibility; reliance on technology removes personality

- **VAs can't communicate complex ideas; personality and message can't come from VAs**

8:

HOW TO MAKE THE KILLER POINT IN PRESENTATIONS AND AVOID SNATCHING DEFEAT FROM THE JAWS OF VICTORY

'When you've spoken the word, it reigns over you.
When it is unspoken, you reign over it.'
Arabian Proverb

We've spent a good deal of time covering the techniques to ensure that your presentations are well-constructed and well-delivered, so that you can achieve a dependable consistency. Unfortunately, as I'm sure you're all too aware, it is possible for a presentation to be immaculately crafted and performed with considerable style and yet not achieve the desired outcome. Why is this, and what are the dynamics that can cause two equally excellent presentations to differ spectacularly in their end results?

Let's return to the idea of receiver-driven communications. What is it that the audience *needs* you to communicate? If you don't touch on this with your presentation, however slick your construction and elegant your delivery, you might just miss the whole point.

We all know the myopia that can accompany being invited to make a presentation on a particular subject. We interpret what we believe to be the needs and requirements of the brief and settle upon a way of answering them. As discussed earlier, this is not unlike making up our minds about our response to a particular question when it is only halfway through being asked, and not listening beyond that point. We drop into transmit mode rather than maintaining a listening perspective. We may hit on the correct answer. But it's just as possible that we will not. Objectivity and the maintenance of a broad, rather than narrow, focus can be a tricky balance to strike; after all, to ensure that our solution or proposal convinces the audience requires a dedication that might make us seem insensitive, or allow us to miss the key point from the audience's perspective. Yes, we need to have conviction about our own case, but not at the cost of consideration for those listening to us.

The point I am trying to make might seem somewhat academic, so I have consulted my historical file of advertising agency presentations. This contains examples of successful as well as unsuccessful outcomes, and although in all cases great care had been taken in the construction and delivery, it was in the understanding of what the client *really wanted to hear*, rather than what the agency really wanted to say, that the key to success resided. Let me illustrate.

How to take account of client sensibilities . . . or not

Getting inside a client's prejudices is an essential function of advertising-account handlers, marketing executives and relationship managers. Knowing all about those personal dislikes and phobias can be instrumental in running a smooth and effective client relationship. But it's essential to keep reviewing the situation in case a previously undiscovered or unnoticed belief makes an appearance.

Into the experience of many, if not all, admen and adwomen will at some time come the Pet-food Account. The third-party, out-of-body experience of appealing to pets' preferences via their owners has a peculiar influence on those involved in marketing and advertising. Spillers had for many years successfully marketed Winalot, the brand leader in dog biscuits, and J. Walter Thompson had, for some time, been the agent for the company's pet-food brands. Then both agency and client teams saw new faces arrive, and what had previously been a relaxed relationship grew unsettled. This coincided with the need for a fresh TV campaign for Winalot and, not surprisingly, the new agency team struggled to resolve the brief. Finally, however, they believed they'd got a winning commercial.

Because of what had become a testy relationship between client and agency teams, the deeper understanding of the client's fixations and foibles had not been getting sufficient attention. Again, the preparation, rehearsals, logic-flow and creative assessment had been spot on. What was lacking was a solid and positive all-round relationship with the man who mattered: the head of marketing, who was able to say yes to the proposals. The critical moment arrived for the theme of the presentation and the strapline on all the advertising to be revealed: 'A dog cannot live by meat alone'. Jaws dropped on the client side of the table. With a bit more commitment to researching our client, rather than nursing concerns about mutual unhappiness, we would have unearthed the fact that this head man was a dedicated Christian who saw our line as blasphemous. Our work had been a waste, because we hadn't realized a funda-mental preconditioning consideration. Digging deeper can often prevent you from digging your own grave.

Getting to understand the client before committing to the expense of actually making proposals can be a cost-effective strategy. As we discussed earlier, listening skills – which allow you to distinguish what the audience wishes to hear about from what you wish to tell them – are an essen-tial part of creating effective presentations. They greatly increase the potential for a successful sale. They also give you the chance to conclude that a particular opportunity has little hope of bearing fruit, and that your efforts would be better placed elsewhere.

Toronto's major audio retailer was a company aptly, as it turned out, called RadioShack. As an agency hungry for business that could turn over a substantial media budget on a regular basis, we were happy to pitch – even though it was a retail account with lots of small ads featuring a discount price on a particular item. We contrived to convince our-selves that we'd be able to talk them into a brand rather than a retail campaign. The obligatory 'factory' visit required a trip north of the city, which turned into something of a journey of discovery.

After about sixty miles on the Queen Elizabeth Highway, my colleague and I were despairing of finding the HQ of our potential client. However, just before we gave up, we managed to spot a rundown cluster of buildings nestling a few hundred yards off the highway, one of which sported a half-lit sign that read 'Rad   ack'. It had to be, and indeed was, our destination. Our potential client met us, and we suspected that the 120-mile round trip might not prove as productive as we'd hoped, when he immediately launched into a diatribe against airy-fairy creative playboys who wanted to waste his money. This impression was reinforced when, on the tour, the client turned out to be completely uninterested in the products he sold and only concerned with ensuring he got as many small ads as possible per $1,000 of expenditure.

The most interesting insight he offered was the description of those *not* in his target market, those with a knowledge of hi-fi who he called 'audiopiles', as they were members of the 'audiopile market'. When we mumbled that they might be called 'audiophiles', we were met with a wrinkled brow and a troubled expression. His target market, he blundered on, were those who knew nothing about hi-fi and who only wanted the cheapest kit to play their 'greatest hits' compilations on. Half an hour in this potential client's company was enough to tell us that we were most definitely in the despised 'audiopile' camp, and that we should make our exit.

How to ensure you're talking to the right person

It might sometimes be the case that the client or audience you are addressing are not who you think they are, that the people you are trying to convince might not be the people who can actually say yes. A certain duplicity has its place in making successful presentations. At Saatchis we had been given the Silk Cut cigarette account without actually presenting any creative work. The agency teams were full of vim and vigour, wanting to get to work on a groundbreaking campaign for the brand. A strategy was agreed with the client team and soon the lights were burning late in the creative department. After several months the body of work had built up, and the client team anticipated an epoch-making change in cigarette advertising.

What we didn't know was that we represented, in fact, a well-designed and executed feinting movement whose role was to distract attention from the development of the actual campaign to be presented. Charles Saatchi, co-founder of Saatchi and Saatchi, and Paul Arden, the agency's eccentric creative director, had been secretly working on a unique and groundbreaking visual idea and they needed time to develop the photography. Our role was to keep the client busy while Charles and Paul fine-tuned the campaign dreamed up whilst having dinner with the company chairman, when a picture had been drawn on a napkin which had landed the account. Eventually we were handed the campaign as a complete package and told to sell it, still unaware that it was something the most senior client had already seen and approved. We were to convince the client's marketing team that the stuff we presented was a work of genius that completely answered their brief, even though they'd been expecting something completely different, along the lines we'd been talking about for several months.

A wonderfully crafted set-piece presentation was put together, and the usual Balkan peace-conference meeting set up. There were even seats for Maurice and Charles Saatchi, but they hadn't attended any formal client presentation in years and made no exception here. Nevertheless the presentation proceeded and was rapturously received. The client team returned to their offices apparently in high spirits. The next day the agency management were hauled over the coals for conning the client, and the presentation team leader, whose pitch had been such a tour de force, was summarily removed, as the most senior available fall guy. However, it has to be said that the agency got the work it wanted approved, the client team accepted they'd been out-manoeuvred, the campaign quadrupled the brand share and ran until all cigarette advertising was banned several years later. The moral of the story: when you're leading a major presentation, be sure you know who your allies are!

How to ensure you present at the best of times

In competitive presentations, where there are several companies making alternative proposals for one piece of business, the timing and location of the presentation can, as we know, be vital. It might sound a minor issue, but the positioning of your pitch in the order of competing companies can seriously affect the chances for success. Pitching for the Barclays International account at Young & Rubicam taught me a lot about timing.

There had been a period of several months between the original client briefing and the suggested dates for presentation by the various agencies involved. This time-lapse had been extended to allow for the agency teams to do their due diligence, contact the various client departments and complete their information-gathering. The Barclays building was a veritable hive of activity with hot-and-cold-running account teams from the various competing agencies crawling about for months on end. Finally all the visits had been made, the analysis of the findings absorbed and the finishing touches put to the agency's creative proposals. The timing for our agency's presentation had been overlooked by the head of our account team and so when the client was approached, we ended up being the last agency to present and we were scheduled for 3 p.m. on a Friday afternoon. If there's a graveyard slot, we'd certainly copped it.

The day dawned and being in July, it dawned hot. The Y&R offices had no air-conditioning and by early afternoon were pretty intolerable. When the client group to whom we were to present arrived, it looked as if they'd had more than a sandwich at their desks to fortify themselves for their afternoon's mental exertions. It was around the halfway mark, just before the creative part of the presentation, that the first head nodded. Now, the odd nodding head, especially in afternoon meetings, need not be anything to worry about. However, within a few minutes, all heads on the client side were down and stayed down, complete with the occasional muted rumble of snoring. The sun shone through the window, and the hum of traffic combined with the snoring of the clients and the buzzing of the bees to make a soporific concert. Manfully we continued to present away, despite the lack of any receiver-driven response . . .

Finally, one of the members of the client team lifted his head to look at the agency team, blinked with a hint of embarrassment, and let out a loud cough which had the effect of rousing the others. Realizing there was no way of rescuing the lost cause, we drew a rapid end to our misery and asked if there were any questions. After a very long silence as the client team wracked their brains for something insightful to say, they finally managed to ask what we thought of the slogan 'Bark with Banclays'. We were forced to conclude that it is hard to win over a client who is asleep, and that the purpose of our presentation had been no more than to make up the numbers. To ensure that you don't have this experience, you must lobby to obtain a satisfactory slot – which means being *neither first nor last*, but second or third, for preference.

How not to gain the attention of a distracted audience

A very famous, even notorious, New York ad agency called Della Femina Travisano & Partners was renowned for taking no prisoners when it came to making presentations. Their President, Jerry Della Femina, known as the Madman of Madison Avenue, was dedicated in his defence of the agency's recommendations, and there were regular occasions where potential and existing clients came away from successful presentations feeling battered if not bruised. The agency grew to match the size of its clients, but size in terms of presentation teams doesn't necessarily mean quality. It just means more potential for distractions.

This was the case with one particular client presentation. The various preambles, marketing, strategy and creative setup had all taken place satisfactorily. Della Femina, with his distinctive shaven head, fearsome beard and dark glasses, then launched into his sale of the creative proposals. He gave a tour de force of insightful understanding of the consumer and their motivations, followed by exciting and impactful advertising proposals, after which he sat down to a respectful round of applause from the client team and asked if they'd got any questions. A middle-ranking client team member asked a perfectly reasonable question of Della Femina, whose reply was interrupted from some way down his own side of the table by a junior agency team member, who fielded the question with what he thought was a better response. While this team member was speaking, Della Femina stood up, walked towards him and punched him right out of his chair. The deathly silence that followed was, after an impressive 'got it?' pause, broken by Della Femina saying, 'As I'm sure you will have grasped, my ex-colleague's view is not that of the agency.'

While the distraction was a costly one for the now unconscious account man, Della Femina had certainly focussed the attention of the client team and could be sure they'd pay serious attention to anything further he might have to say! While such extreme antics might be excusable in eccentric company owners, today's employment lawyers would certainly take a dim and expensive view. However, this is a good cautionary tale for your presentation team colleagues, when warning them about the wisdom of interruptions.

How *not* to identify impactful concrete examples to animate your presentation

In order for your presentation to be in the form of a conversation, we have seen that it is essential to use everyday examples that your audience can understand and relate to. You should be careful, however, that you don't overdo the analogy or, as illustrated in the following case, its concrete quality. This is a KMP story, and relates to the time they were presenting proposals to the English Butter Marketing Company, a new consortium of the then Milk Marketing Board, for the Country Life butter brand developed to compete with Kerrygold and Anchor, from Ireland and New Zealand respectively.

These were the days when 'creativity' was accorded more respect than it is in the pragmatic, even prosaic, climate of today. Again, by talking to the client as well as to the dairy farmers, and by doing some anecdotal research amongst housewives, the agency team came up with the basis for their creative proposals. They believed that the target consumers of Country Life butter needed to be put back in touch with their rural roots. All of this from a bunch of creative johnnies in the Wild West End of London, whose only sight of the countryside was when they flew over it on the way to a Caribbean holiday.

Determined to bring their presentation alive to the equally urban client team, a central visual of a milkmaid with butter churns and a contented-looking English milking cow was developed. The presentation focussed whole-heartedly on Englishness, countryside and what the team began to refer to as 'the factory' (by which they meant the cow). This is where the gap between the natural enthusiasm of creative talent and the constraints of reality began to widen; a gap where the account-handling team, guardians of the client relationship, should have stepped in. The creative team had decided it was essential to have an example of 'the factory' in the presentation to bring their idea alive.

The KMP offices were in a high-rise building near Leicester Square, on the eighth floor. The lifts were normally adequate but were not the monster ones we're used to today. Fitting a cow into one of these lifts presented an almost insurmountable problem, only overcome by perseverance, a persuasive dairy farmer and a very placid cow. The office cleaning company, however, cancelled their contract the following day. But the 'factory', in all of its glory, was brought to life in the small conference room. Suffice to say the heat, the occasion, and the stress of stardom all worked their influence on the cow who, after all, was just a poor country girl. Luckily, the results of her stressful day were not apparent until the client had departed – having bought the agency's presentation! I would always recommend creating your own concrete examples, and if you do delegate to the creative department then conduct an early reality check.

The above are admittedly some of the more amusing ways in which to deliver, or not, killer points to presentations. However hard you try, happenstance will creep into even the best-planned efforts, and one of the most important attributes is a sense of the ridiculous and a well-honed sense of humour.

Summary

- **Make sure the audience's deeper motivations have been considered**

- **Objectivity, and broad rather than narrow focus**

- **In synthesizing the key elements of the presentation be sympathetic to your audience**

- **Ensure you present key proposals to those who can say yes**

- **Everything's fair in love and presentations!**

- **Always be sure who your allies are**

- In competitive presentations, where and when you present are vital

- Lobby hard to ensure favourable treatment

- Beware careless interruptions from colleagues

- Keep control of your own material

9:

MEDIA TRAINING AND CRISIS MANAGEMENT

'Any idiot can face a crisis – it's day-to-day living that wears you out.'
Anton Chekhov

We've all felt a delicious shudder down our spines as we see or hear someone we've little time for being skewered by an interviewer like Jeremy Paxman, John Humphrys or some of the other forensic operators in broadcast media. Similarly, we'll occasionally have hugged ourselves as we read an interview in the press where the subject has managed to offer up some serious hostage to fortune, clearly having not spotted their interviewer leading them into an elephant trap. It's not often that we're told a politician or organization has 'declined the opportunity' to appear for an interview and, presumably, a sound roasting. Yet time and again we hear of politicians and businessmen being neatly stitched up by walking, apparently eyes-wide-open, into a hostile interview environment.

There are strong forces at work here, and pretty massive egos. An invitation to appear on *Today* or *Newsnight*, with the attendant possibility of impressing a national audience with a readily achieved flawless delivery of a complex message, is generally impossible to refuse.

We've talked about the essential aspects of making an effective presentation, as well as the issue of answering difficult questions. Yet time after time, we see and hear interviewees enthusiastically breaking all the basic rules and ending up well and truly filleted by their media nemeses. Why won't they learn? Do they live in an atmosphere of such limited self-criticism that even abject failure becomes characterized as success?

Unfortunately, media interviews, and hostile ones at that, are meat and drink for the modern politician and high-end civil servants. Only by adhering to the sort of key aspects of spoken communications I've laid out can they avoid, as far as possible, coming across as unimpressive under media scrutiny. As with crisis management – and the two issues do have considerable overlap – it's possible to find training organizations that can help with the pitfalls discussed above.

In the event that you find yourself shouldering responsibility for dealing with media relations or indeed crisis management itself, I would strongly suggest that you insist on your organization investing in some specific training for the task they've charged you with. There are a number of consultancies, listed at the end of this book, whose focus is on training executives for media interviews and dealing with the media in crisis situations.

Media training takes the form of being interviewed by a current media figure employed for this purpose by the company. They'll use video playback to demonstrate how successful or unsuccessful you've been in meeting the two basic objectives of getting both your message and your personality across. In our highly professional modern media environment, there is, quite simply, far too much at stake in terms of effective message delivery to leave anything to chance.

Dealing with the media is a high-risk game and you need all the support you can get.

Crisis management

The importance of effective crisis management

A few years ago there was a horrendous air crash where a British Midland plane landed on a motorway, killing several motorists and many passengers. The chairman of the airline was door-stepped by the press and TV cameras before there'd been time to brief him about the accident. It would have been entirely possible for him to blurt out some ill-considered facts or comments, putting the reputation of his company at stake and causing untold upset to relatives of the casualties from the crash. Instead he firmly refused to answer any question about details of the disaster until he'd received a proper briefing, but he offered himself up for interview on the next major news bulletin. In the meantime he received the required briefing, enabling him to answer questions properly and informatively, rather than muddling through and looking less than in control of the situation. The company's reputation and share price didn't suffer any damage. In fact their handling of the crisis added to their reputation rather than detracting from it.

The other end of the crisis-management spectrum was the impact on BP's share price, and the subsequent development of punitive claims against them, as a result of their poor handling of a hugely hostile US-media response to an oil-rig explosion. Here an off-the-cuff remark by a senior manager about sailing with his family caused a reaction that was harmful to the company, since the death toll had not, at that point, been established.

If you are the first-up responder on behalf of your organization, it's likely you will have been trained to ensure you don't fall into the sort of traps mentioned. In the event that you haven't received any training, it would be advisable, given the huge costs of corporate disasters, to do so without delay.

The ins and outs of crisis management

In 2015 we followed an unfolding horror story of corporate poor judgement. The Volkswagen crisis over their misrepresentation of diesel emissions is a shining example of how not to handle a problem. A local difficulty became a worldwide catastrophe. The continuing crisis at VW shows that no corporation, however large, whatever political influence they wield or however much money they can throw at the problem, is immune from being punished for misdeeds. No matter what their size and importance, if the company does not, *from the start,* employ the right strategy for handling the crisis, and implement it with dedication and consistency, the effects can be catastrophic.

Having made the mistake of lying about emissions tests for its diesel cars in the world's most punitive market, VW has seen its share price decimated and the corporation's future put at considerable risk. While the chief executive may, laudably, have fallen on his sword, one top-level executive's scalp did little to quieten the baying for blood from the media and disgruntled VW stakeholders. In the era of social media, the efforts of the corporation to calm public opinion have been dreadful, with customers and stakeholders remaining lamentably under-informed about the company's intentions to resolve matters. The timings, details and legalities of the problems caused by the original statements were, and remain, opaque, in a manner that the media and other interested parties do not applaud.

Above all, you always need a plan

It is hard to believe, in a world driven by high-speed communications, that some major corporations don't have a strategy or plan to deal with the sorts of calamities that make regular headlines in today's business press. Don't their managements read the papers or watch the TV? Are they too cocooned from reality to realize that they have to pay continuous attention to the image of the corporate entity for which they're responsible? How might they prepare, when they eventually wake up, for the problems that could arise for their particular company?

There's a crying need for corporations to put in place contingency plans. While they may well have effective plans to deal with, say, the physical effects of an air crash or a factory exploding, they haven't thought about the communications implications of the crisis, as it moves from actual occurrence phase to aftermath phase. That's when the costs of getting it wrong can really start to escalate.

A client – the chief executive of a large, high-profile charity, who is also a non-executive director of a number of private-sector corporations – said to me recently that the role of a chief executive in today's unforgiving business world is to be on call 24 hours a day, 365 days a year, without any possible respite. As the corporation's first line of defence, CEOs must be ready to field whatever happens to be thrown at them in the middle of the night, or whenever they step into the limelight by design or default. My client was beginning to find the pressure of the role intolerable and had been seeking to move to a number of consultative positions, enabling him to remove himself from the immediate firing line. He's not yet fifty!

In the recent case of the Malaysian Airlines disaster, the missing Flight MH370, the company was lambasted by the Chinese state media and a long list of other commentators for delaying thirteen hours before announcing the disappearance of the flight and the actions the airline proposed to take. Subsequent lack of transparency towards the relatives of the victims of the crash caused further outrage, and the incompetence of the management peaked when they finally informed the relatives of the certainty of their loss by text message. It's hard to conceive of how the crisis could have been handled in a worse fashion, and the result of this incompetence was a massive hit to the commercial value as well as the reputation of the airline, leaving it now virtually dead in the water. If only they'd paid minimal attention to the basic rules of effective communication.

Don't panic. Don't cover up and whatever you do don't be economical with the truth.

Right person, right place, right time, right response

The chief executive must take immediate responsibility for any major crisis. It's simply not good enough for the first line of defence to be a spokesperson of indeterminate seniority.

We've all sat open-mouthed in front of our TVs as some poor minion who's drawn the short straw fumbles their way through a media presentation that should have been the responsibility of those at the top of the organization. The buck stops at the top and for the drama to be contained, control must be seized and retained.

A chief executive calmly dealing with a media grilling and expressing genuine concern for the affected parties offers an immediate reassurance that the organization is in control of the situation and is handling the problem effectively. Ownership of the crisis has been established. Unfortunately too many senior executives take the line of attempting to reassure the stakeholders, the media, and the public that the company is still to be trusted, when it's quite obvious that it can't be. The time for the issue of reputation to be attended to is after the crisis has been effectively handled, not when it's still at the red-hot stage. The media and stakeholders are simply not interested in bland reassurance when firm and decisive action is required. Playing off the back foot ends up undermining corporate and executive credibility. *Once a senior company representative is on the hook, wriggling isn't an option.*

A masterclass in getting it wrong was given when the chief executive of a hotel company appeared on TV, faced with over 100 specific complaints about the cleanliness of one of his hotels. He started off by claiming that the *vast majority* of the company's properties were just fine, showing a flagrant disregard for the customers' findings and revealing that he was only concerned for the already ruined reputation of his firm.

Another hospitality company, Thomas Cook, also got themselves into hot water with their recent inability to say sorry. Having delayed commenting until they were declared liable for the deaths of two children in one of their holiday apartments, it wasn't until nearly nine years later that they finally apologized to the bereaved parents. After a period of sustained criticism, the company's chief executive had to publicly confess that it had been his 'biggest mistake'.

It's easy to underestimate how difficult it can be to take control, and maintain control, of the rolling media circus that accompanies every high-profile crisis or disaster. Communicating quickly and effectively will always require rapid responses that aren't always completely thought through. Lawyers and other specialists tend to be concerned only that their particular area of expertise is not subject to misrepresentation and they don't end up being scapegoated.

All too often the person dealing with the media isn't in possession of all the necessary information, all of the time. In which case, by far the best decision they can take is to say nothing. Generally, although not always, if this silence is handled properly the media will be prepared to accept that there's no necessity for chief executives, chairmen or other spokespeople to dig their own graves. But they do require them to bear responsibility and to show some understanding of events. So again, a demonstration of the power of silence.

Is it possible to recover from such events?

Companies have recovered from major, even catastrophic, assaults on their reputations. Committing to investing large sums while the share price remains considerably depressed following a rocky period does require serious nerve on the part of management and shareholders. In the harsh light of post-crisis judgement, the choice is to either show yourself to have wholeheartedly adopted the requirements of public opinion, or to accept that a pre-eminent reputation has been fundamentally and irrevocably tarnished and thus behave accordingly. In the case of VW, this would mean reviewing what had been a previously peerless reputation as a responsible manufacturer, and changing strategic direction to accommodate a future in which they will occupy a more functional and prosaic position.

High-reputation brands and franchises can, nevertheless, prove resilient with sensitive handling. After experiencing reputational problems with some of its product introductions, Apple bounced back with subsequent product successes. The furore that arose after the discovery of problems with working conditions in the factories of their Chinese suppliers soon died down due to transparency in the company's response. A carefully maintained and burnished reputation for good corporate governance and communications can pay very serious dividends when faced with a short-term reputational knock.

This continuing success in crisis and reputation management was brought about by corporate management doing exactly what we've been discussing throughout this book: they founded their response in effective presentation techniques. First of all they listened and ensured they knew what the problem really was. Next, they formulated a relevant and focussed strategy founded in the communication of factual rebuttals of the negative storylines from the press. Finally they focussed on one man to lead the effort and he remained consistently on top of his brief. Apple remains one of the cash-richest corporations in the world, with a share-price performance that makes many other major corporations extremely jealous. And it's not surprising that when an individual gets his corporation's message and personality across effectively, it does a power of good to both his career and his standing in the business world.

Public opinion can be made to change its mind. If we believe corporations to be genuinely contrite, we can be quite forgiving – especially where the corporation has clearly got a planned and effective response. Conversely, those companies and senior executives that dither, take their time and are seen to have to have concessions dragged unwillingly out of them, continue to suffer reputational damage long after the original crisis has passed. The planned responses of Apple and other effectively communicating corporations have continually borne fruit.

Crisis management founded in sound spoken communications lends credibility to corporations and their leaders.

Putting a plan together

1. Start with the basics

Whoever you are talking to, whether a customer, a shareholder, a journalist, a regulator or a legislator, your communications should be, *as always*, receiver-driven. More than ever, in such extreme circumstances, it's essential your audience understands your message and is given sufficient time to absorb it.

2. Look at all aspects of operations

Needless to say, each crisis will be different, although how your organization addresses the particular issues may, in fact, be treated very similarly. An effective crisis-management plan requires all areas of an organization's operations to be scrutinized, along with the development of crisis scenarios which will accommodate possible events. For example, using VW as an illustration, all aspects of manufacture, labour relations, marketing, regulation, non-domestic operations and competitive activity as specific sources of crisis relating to each individual area, would need to be reviewed. Of course, VW may well have thought they'd done just that, but unfortunately the execution of the plan, if it existed, was hopeless.

3. Identify the key players

The point when crisis strikes is not the time for having a casting session to decide who in senior management would be the best person to represent the face of the corporation. The horse has already bolted. From the start of creating the plan, the people charged with executing it have to be involved. This group, at the very least, should include the chairman, chief executive, finance director and communications/PR director. Any one of these figures should be able to pick up the plan at the start of the crisis and be capable of running with it to manage the situation.

4. Rehearse regularly

Worse than having no plan at all is to draw one up and then put it in a drawer to await the collapse of the world around your ears. Once drawn up, the plan needs to be rehearsed in detail with the group identified above. The group needs to be large enough to always have at least one member readily available and capable of getting on a plane to overseas locations if called upon. Inevitably, the actual crisis is unlikely to be identical to the ones rehearsed, but if the construction of possible scenarios has been done effectively, there will be sufficient similarities to enable the creation of an effective first-line response.

5. Review regularly

The world has an unfortunate habit of turning and requiring us to turn with it. The best-laid plans of today may well look inappropriate a year or two down the line. It's essential to take out the plan every few months and check that it still fits possible events, especially in the light of what may have been happening in the arenas in which the organization operates. It may well be necessary to rewrite and re-rehearse the whole plan and possibly even change the personnel identified to lead. It's not an effective crisis-management plan if it doesn't have the capacity to adapt successfully while still meeting the original objectives set for it at inception.

6. Get objective input

In general, it's not that great a strategy to keep your cards unnecessarily close to your chest. Limiting the process of planning to a tight internal corporate group can be potentially dangerous, with managements being all too prone to talking to themselves and listening to their own reassurances. Using outside consultants or experts in the field can provide both a valuable objectivity and an effective editing and revising function. External advisers can also, in the event of an actual crisis, act as an invaluable, ready-briefed resource.

7. *Take the offensive when necessary and possible*

The natural tendency of any corporation finding itself under intense scrutiny or criticism is to revert to being defensive. Not every crisis is of the corporation's own making. 'Events, dear boy, events,' as Harold Macmillan supposedly said, can cause things to go off track. Macmillan was famously good at avoiding awkward questions, but finally fell from power because he wouldn't ask sufficiently difficult questions of his own, especially of John Profumo, which resulted in a major and very messy political scandal.

There'll always be occasions where blame is incorrectly apportioned and it's necessary to robustly rebut a line of unfair or unreasonable questioning. Interested parties will generally be perfectly prepared to accept a firm denial or rebuttal, but only if the supporting evidence is correctly put to them without rancour or aggression, however forcefully the question itself might have been posed. However, where the crisis has arisen because of a sin of commission on the part of a corporation, then the strategy has to be to maximize a perception of openness, candidness and preparedness to do what is necessary to satisfactorily resolve the issue. Muddled interviews, smokescreens, evading clear questions and general shiftiness are the worst possible ways to approach managing a crisis.

Summary

Dealing with real life is far more testing than dealing with theory. What's clear from the various experiences described above is how much easier it is to get it wrong than to get it right. But, as has been shown, there are corporations who've successfully ridden out the storms of publicity and come through with their reputations either unharmed or even, on occasion, enhanced. So it's worthwhile underlining the key things they got right:

- Develop a corporate crisis-management plan

- Identify the key personnel to be involved

- Rehearse the plan

- Review the plan regularly

- Take outside objective advice

- Respond to each crisis on its merits

- Keep faith with the plan

The last point I wish to make is to emphasize the need, once all the processes for producing and regularly reviewing the plan have been gone through, not to throw it out of the window at the moment of crisis. One final word of cautious realism: however much preparation is done, however water-tight everything looks, nothing ever goes totally to plan. An awareness that all crises are unique is something worth keeping in mind at all times, as is a determination to keep faith with the basic techniques of effective spoken communications that we've covered in this book.

CONCLUSION

'I am turned into a sort of machine for observing facts and grinding out conclusions.'
Charles Darwin

I hope I've convinced you of the necessity to approach all forms of verbal communications with care, and that I've established with you a greater understanding of what makes for successful communication. It's remarkable how often, and in how many circumstances, the need to apply some of the lessons I've outlined becomes necessary. While not wanting to give the impression that every situation is effectively a presentation, much of what we say is heavily dependent on how we say it. The vast majority of our lives at home and at work are spent dealing with others, and generally this is achieved through face-to-face conversations, which, from time to time, become more complex and structured. So, while the circumstances may change, the fundamentals of the activity remain the same.

In the same way that children can develop different patterns of behaviour at school and at home, we adults communicate differently in different environments. We'd never raise our voices at work colleagues in the way that, for instance, we might be tempted to with our children or even, dare I suggest, our husbands, wives or partners. Yet do we ever stop to consider the effectiveness of such communications? If I've managed to convince you that all spoken communication is receiver-driven, the demarcation between various audiences and the ways in which we deliver our spoken messages should no longer exist. Every word we speak, other than the occasional mutterings of frustration, is aimed at others, and is usually an attempt to engage them in some action or thought process.

Of course it's going to take time and practice before the lessons covered in the previous chapters become an instinctive part of your communication and presentation habits. I believe that it's an effort not only worth making, but that these lessons are essential in order to effectively communicate with the world around us. Which is, after all, fundamental to our business and personal development, isn't it?

Useful Organizations

Crisis-management consultancies

- www.visorconsultants.com
- www.issue-crisis.com
- www.regesterlarkin.com

Media-interview training consultancies

- www.simply-speaking.co.uk
- www.mediatrainingassociates.co.uk

*Illustrations by Dan Colman – one of
my mentors on effective communications*

Index

adrenalin 7, 8, 14, 15, 23, 30
Apple 123, 124
Attlee, Clement 13
audience:
    conversation with, presentation
        as 6–7, 8, 11, 14–17, 19–21,
        23, 25, 27–8
    distracted 109–10
    empathy and 16, 19
    holding your 27–8
    see also under individual area of
        presentation
autocue 24, 70

Barclays International 107–9
'bathtub diagram' (speaking technique
    illustration) 68
'bits'/'bites', compression of
    information into 28, 34, 67–8
Boeing 48
Bonaparte, Napoleon 30
BP 117–18
British Airways 44
British Midland 117

camera, recording presentations to
    20, 31–2, 33, 69
central focus, presentation 17–19
Chekhov, Anton 115
Churchill, Winston 45
client sensibilities 102–5
communications:
    receiver-driven 20, 26, 27, 80, 101,
        108, 124, 130

    theory of 10, 27–8
consistency, how to achieve 23–36
    avoid reading set texts 23–4
    holding your audience 27–8
    information compression 27–9
    methodology, a proposed 29–36
    time, importance of 25–7
construct your presentation, how
    to 37–57
    content 45–56 *see also* content,
        refining presentation
    strategy 37–42 *see also* strategy,
        presentation
    structure 42–5 *see also* structure,
        refining presentation
content, refining presentation 45–56
    distractions, avoiding 53–5
    examples, use of 47–9
    humour 50
    key messages 45
    main content 46–7
    personal style and tone 49
    start, strong 50–3
    visual aids 56
conversational style:
    effective communication and
        6–7, 11, 14–17, 19–21, 23, 2
        5, 27–30, 31, 34, 35, 68, 71,
        110
    examples and 110
    nature of conversation and 19–21,
        27–9, 31–2, 34
    notes and 71
    pausing and *see* pauses

conversational style (*cont.*):
    Q&A and 83, 86
    recoding your 31–2, 34–5
    stage techniques and 29–30, 34
    timing and 25
crisis management 117–28
    chief executive and timing of
        response 120–2
    importance of effective 117–18
    poor judgement in 118–19
    recovery from crisis 122–4
    plan, need of 119–20
    plan, putting together a 124–7
        basics 124
        key players, identify the 125
        look at all aspects of
            operations 124–5
        objective input 126
        rehearse regularly 125–6
        review regularly 126
        take the offensive when
            necessary and possible 127

Darwin, Charles 129
deliver your presentation, how
    to 59–65
    detail, be a stickler for 63–5
    rehearsal 59–60
    setup and location 63
    sticking to the script 61–3
    timing 60–1
delivery methods 44–5, 67–78
    see also notes and headings *and* set
        text/script
detail, be a stickler for 63–5
distracted audience 109–10
distractions, avoiding 53–5

empathy, audience and 16, 19
engagement, signs of 27, 61
Eurotunnel 97–8
examples:
    how not to identify 110–12
    use of 11, 47–9

formality:
    effects of upon performance 13–14
    lighting and 98
    set text/script and 67–9
    tone and 16, 20–1

holding your audience 27–8
humour 50, 112

information-compression 28–9

J. Walter Thompson 103

key messages 45, 56
key principles, some 9–22
    central focus of your
        presentation 17–19
    conversation with your audience 6,
        14–21
    empathy, audience and 16, 19
    formality and 13–14
    get your personality across 12–13
    getting your message across 10–12
    key objectives 9–12
killer point 62, 112
KMP 110–12

length of presentation 42–3, 61
Levi-Strauss, Claude 79
light, room 64, 65, 95–6, 98
listening, Q&A and 80–1
location 63–4

main content 46–7
Malaysian Airlines MH370 120
media training 115–17
messages:
    getting your message across 10–12
    key 45, 56
methodology, a proposed 29–36

nerves 7, 12, 14–15, 76
notes and headings 71–8
    familiarity of 71

format of 76–7
length of 73–4
note cards 76
personal nature of 71–3
route map, as a dependable 74–5
seamless flow, ensuring a 76
visual aids and 77–8

objectively, speaking 9–12
off the cuff, speaking 88–9
over-answering, Q&A and 82–3

pacing 25–7
pauses 5
    advanced technique 67–9
    'bathtub diagram' and 68
    'consideration' 32–5, 69, 83, 84
    'got it?' 32–5, 68, 69, 84, 85, 110
    length of 28
    notes and 76
    as punctuation 26
    Q&A and 82–3, 84, 85
    set text and 68, 69
    techniques 29–35, 67–9
persistent questioner, Q&A and 85–6
personal style and tone 49
personality, communicating your:
    crisis management and 124
    key objective of presentation 9, 10,
        12–13, 16
    media training and 116
    Q&A and 79, 80–1
    room lighting and 96, 98
    visual aids and 92, 93, 99
planning:
    crisis management and 119–20,
        124–8
    practice and 40–2
    starting early 38–40
    taking seriously 37–8
PowerPoint 77–8, 91
practice see rehearsal
preparation and strategy 37–42

getting your planning started
    early 38–40
practice and 40–2
taking the planning seriously 37–8
'presentation speak' 16, 20–1

question-and-answer sessions 79–90
    ending/length of 87
    if you don't know, admit it 84–5
    listening 80–1
    long and involved questions 86–7
    over-answering 82–3
    persistent questioner 85–6
    rushing to answer 84
    speaking off the cuff 88–9
    treading carefully 79–80

rehearsal:
    autocue and 70
    constructing presentation and 41,
        42
    crisis management and 125–6
    humour and 50
    importance of 1, 3, 4, 15, 59–60
    methodology and 31–2
    notes and 74, 103
    script and 63, 69, 71
    visual aids and 56, 94, 97
repetition 22, 44, 45, 65
right person, ensure you're talking to
    the 105–7
rushing to answer, Q&As and 84

Saatchi & Saatchi 105–7
scope 42
script see set text/script
seamless flow, ensuring a 76
set text/script 67–71
    advanced technique 67–9
    autocue 70
    avoid reading 23–4
    methodology and 31, 32
    sticking to the 61–3
setup and location 63, 65

signposts for audience, creating 47, 54
simplicity:
    examples and 47–9
    message 10–12, 45
    visual aids and 94–5, 98
slides:
    development of 91, 93–4
    lasting impressions and 97–8
    lighting and 96, 97–8
    opening with 53–4, 96
    PowerPoint and 77–8
    preferred type of 94–5
    problems with 3–4
    see also visual aids
Sophocles 67
start, strong 50–3, 54–5, 93, 96
stress 7, 8, 14, 15, 16, 23, 30, 32, 112
structure, refining presentation 42–5
    delivery method 44–5
    length 42–3
    scope 42
    theme 44
style and tone, personal 49

technology, using 64, 96–7, 98–9 see
    also visual aids

theme, unifying 44
Thomas Cook 121–2
time/timing:
    length of presentation 60–1
    pacing, importance of 25–7
    when to present, choosing 107–9
Twain, Mark 12, 29, 29n, 59

visual aids 56, 91–9
    central focus of your presentation
        and 17
    checking 64
    deciding to use 45
    development of 91–4
    lighting and 95–6
    notes and 74
    planning presentation and 38
    refining your presentation structure
        and 56
    slides and see slides
    supporting nature of 96, 97–8
    technology, unreliability of 96–8
Volkswagen (VW) 118–19, 123, 125
von Braun, Werner 10–12

Wilde, Oscar 9